# SAGE-ing While AGE-ing

# SAGE-ing While AGE-ing

## SHIRLEY MacLAINE

SIMON &
SCHUSTER

London · New York · Sydney · Toronto

A CBS COMPANY

First published in Great Britain by Simon & Schuster UK Ltd, 2007
A CBS COMPANY

Published in the US in 2007 by Atria Books,
A Division of Simon & Schuster, Inc.
1230 Avenue of the Americas
New York, NY 10020

*Designed by Joel Avirom and Jason Snyder*

1 3 5 7 9 10 8 6 4 2

Simon & Schuster UK Ltd
Africa House
64–78 Kingsway
London WC2B 6AH

www.simonsays.co.uk

Simon & Schuster Australia
Sydney

A CIP catalogue record for this book
is available from the British Library.

ISBN: 978-1-84737-168-3

Printed and bound in Great Britain by
Mackays of Chatham Ltd

*For Brit and Kevin:*
*thank you all ways*

# Foreword

I HAVE BEEN A QUESTIONER ALL MY LIFE—SOMETIMES irritatingly so. It's my nature to question the nature of nature. What is real? What is hidden? I must have been born with a gene for being open-minded and curious. This impulse has motivated my political values, my creative work, my relationships, and my spiritual search for deeper meaning. Who and what is that creative source, who are we, how did we get here, and where are we going?

This book encompasses a great deal of research that I have done with others who have the same questioning nature. Some of what I write may seem dense, but then we live in a world of density that we don't always understand. I'm looking for a little bit of clarity.

Over the years, I've come to understand and appreciate the value of conflict although I don't like it. But I understand that it is a teacher!

My years in Hollywood have given me an exquisite appreciation of eccentricity and the manipulation of power and perception. For me it was a natural progression to analyze human behavior almost from a DNA point of view. How have we come to be the way we are?

As a person of years, I am concerned more and more with longevity and the connection of mind, body, and spirit. Medicine that addresses itself to healing by way of energy and consciousness has helped me greatly. I don't like drugs or the cut, burn, and poison approach. It is obsolete in most cases anyway. I'll share with you my own experiences with such health issues, particularly dentistry.

I have never felt we are alone in the cosmos, and in the pages that follow I'll address myself to that intuitive belief, as well as present a great deal of credible evidence supporting my views. Some very serious people have shed light on this subject, as you'll see. It is time for the curtain of ridicule, derision, and denial to come down.

Mostly, I'm going to question and share what I have learned relating to our connection to what I call "the God source": the God Within and the God Without. I question what is God and who were "the gods." Why won't our government tell us the truth about visitors from other worlds? Does the military-industrial complex always need to make us afraid of something in order to continue to exist? And, more than anything, I question the nature of fear and what it stems from.

I have spent most of my adult life endeavoring to educate myself in the truths that we are not traditionally taught and do not readily see. I have been privileged to be able to afford to travel around the globe searching out answers to these mystical but fundamentally practical questions in many cultures. I have a vast library of research material with which I am very familiar. It helps me feel less alone in questioning things many are afraid to venture into themselves. I am not an occultist (which simply means "hidden"). I am the opposite. I share everything publicly.

I investigate. I believe deeply in God and feel that this "source" energy resides in everyone—even those we call evil. I don't really understand what "evil" means except that it is "live" spelled backward (which could be a definition in itself).

I believe the great creator intended for all of us to feel happiness. Because of the laws of cause and effect (science as well as karma), each of us has a different road to completion and happiness.

I try to be nonjudgmental on my road to completion, understanding, and happiness and hope that you, dear Reader, will feel the same way. STAY OPEN-MINDED—OTHERWISE THE TRUTH MAY NOT EMERGE. Even truth needs to feel acknowledged!

# chapter

# 1

I'M SITTING ON THE PORCH OF MY NEW HOUSE OVERLOOKING Santa Fe, New Mexico. I'm moving in and I'm exhausted from unpacking boxes, putting up pictures, and ruminating about my life. I do a lot of ruminating these days, but moving into a new house is making it more intense than usual.

The house isn't really new (it's fifteen years old) but it is new to me, and it's a dream place for me.

A house is really a life . . . one you've had or one you want to have. A new dream.

Whenever I have a really good dream, I find it's usually about a house (my life) with new additional rooms (new chapters and adventures) for me to wander through.

Now, as I take a break and look out over the terrain here in the Land of Enchantment I find myself freely associating about my own "inner terrain."

It's a challenge for me to realize that I am older than I thought I was. I feel like a sage-ing "icon" (as the young people call me). I feel I *must* become a sage, or I can't deal with the reality of what we've allowed ourselves to become—me included.

At dinner parties these days the table falls virtually silent when I say something (anything) because the other guests expect a treatise on enlightenment. I'm told I predicted 9/11 and the erratic weather changes a long time ago. I don't remember any of it, but then I don't remember much of anything these days. The day I couldn't remember where I put my car keys was one thing. But when I finally found them and I couldn't remember what they were for, I knew I had reached the age for either sageing or an old folks' home. I picked sageing.

I've decided to believe everything I hear. Why not? It's all unbelievable anyway. I mean, most everything these days challenges what I grew up knowing and believing was a kind of sane truth.

Our president invades a country because Jesus or God told him to. Wow! And people think I'm wacky for believing in other lives and guiding spirits who channel through humans. Wasn't that what happened to W.? "I don't listen to my old man because I have a higher-powered spirit who got me off of heavy-duty 'spirits' along with drugs." Wow again! What should we honestly think about all that? Should we believe him? Maybe so. But who and what were *his* spirits and *his* gods?

Tomorrow I will start hanging family pictures on the walls of my new house. I remember that my father was a serial alcoholic who was intelligent and told the truth. In fact, I respected him for the reasons *why* he drank. He couldn't bear the hypocrisy he saw all around him.

He told me about the out-of-body experience he had when he cracked up the car. He said he went out of his body and met with his own father and mother again. He said he saw the light of God around them and knew that light was his real home. He wanted to go there—into the light—but something stopped him—a voice, maybe, who told him he needed to go back to his life on Earth and finish the work he had agreed to do. He said he had contracted to have his life with our family, and he knew he wasn't finished.

He never told anyone about his experience until I brought home my first metaphysical book which I read to him and Mother. (I always read my books to my parents before I published them.) He was glad to talk to someone about it. I knew how he felt—it had happened to me in Peru when I sat on a mountaintop in the Andes and left my body to witness the Earth below me. Was I crazy, I wondered, or was I liberated from limitations? Dad went on to tell me that he had seen his best buddy appear at the foot of his bed at the exact moment that he died in World War II. I remember asking him if he thought anyone ever really died. He looked at me with a quizzical expression but didn't say anything in reply.

Maybe death is as exciting as life. Maybe war is a karmic dance between the killers and the killees, and no soul ever really dies. If that is so, then what is the point of war? Is the real reason for war to teach us the karmic steps of the dance until we are exhausted by it?

My dad had as many questions as I did. He loved philosophy and psychology. Questions like: Are we alone in the universe? Why are we here? Why are we the way we are? What is energy? Is there life before life?

He always asked himself those questions and never stopped me from asking mine. He was kind of a hometown philosopher.

I loved that about him. He had a hard time understanding why people behaved the way they did, with such subterfuge and hypocrisy. He would always tell the truth, even to his own detriment. For example, during his days selling real estate he would tell a prospective client that the water pump didn't work or a new roof was needed, then wonder why such disclosure blew the sale. He couldn't understand why truth was such a deterrent. He was an educated man who wrote unfinished dissertations on philosophy and psychology at Johns Hopkins. He never finished because he was ridiculed by one of his professors. I remember reading one of his papers on music. In it he said he could prove that notes had the same vibrational frequency as colors. He didn't know then that he was talking about the human chakra system, but he was. And when I told him about the seven notes on the scale corresponding to the seven rainbow colors of the chakra system, he welled up with tears. He was trying to prove something intellectually that he knew was true intuitively. He was very patriotic and used to cry at the "Star-Spangled Banner," too.

Mother was a Canadian by birth and Daddy loved showing her around the Washington Monument, the Capitol, White House, Lincoln Memorial, etc., while she was studying to become a citizen of the United States.

Mother didn't show the emotional passion Daddy did. (She was a Canadian, after all.) Her love was for nature and regrowth in the spring. She said that was why she partially understood the theory of reincarnation. Same soul, different life every rebirth. Same bush, different rose every spring.

Neither of them ridiculed my questions, my expanding

beliefs, or my tendency to expound on such things in public. They used to say, "Well, it could all be true."

Daddy told me he secretly always wanted to run away and join the circus. He was a good musician who played the violin, but turned down a scholarship in Europe because he didn't want to study hard to become a professional musician only to end up playing in the pit of a Broadway musical eight times a week. Hence, later on, he became a real estate salesman. I think I'm good with the value of real estate because of him. My agent used to say that because of my investments in real estate, I have lived rent-free my whole life.

Mother was an artist, an actress, and loved to read poetry. Her mother was the Dean of Women at Acadia University in Wolfville, Nova Scotia, Canada. And Mother's father was a brain surgeon (one of the best in Canada, I'm told) and as I found out later, going through the attic after they both had passed on, her father was a thirty-third-degree Mason! I found newspaper articles that she had saved attesting to that fact, but she never told me herself. Maybe she didn't even know.

She did tell me, though, that she was at her father's side when he died (she was seventeen), and at his passing he said to her, "Oh, it's sooo beautiful. Don't be sorry, it's incredibly beautiful." So I suppose I got my spiritual and metaphysical leanings from both my parents.

I guess we could say that belief is a result of our imagination. But then perhaps we are imagining we are alive, as the Buddhists propound. We dream our lives during the day, and night dream them when we sleep. The trick is to avoid the nightmares of each by understanding who we really are. I've always liked Einstein's quote, "Imagination is more important than knowledge."

As I look back over my life, as my mind wanders freely over how I've lived and loved and protested and questioned, I realize that aging well isn't about the search for happiness, but more about quietly feeling content with what I've experienced. Loving without caring too much, you might say. And more than anything, I've come to appreciate the value of conflict. Everything isn't always meant to be light and love. The dark times, the conflicts, that's where real learning can happen.

For example, during the Great Depression my family never had more than $300 in the bank, and we were taught to save for the future because one never knew when it could happen again. I remember I was confused over the declaration of war I heard Roosevelt announce through the old-fashioned radio in the living room as we gathered around trying to understand what "infamy" meant. I wept over the death of Roosevelt as I was coming up the back stairs of our house in Richmond, Virginia. I loved the "victory gardens" we were taught to till every weekend to be rewarded with ice-cream dinners on Sunday nights.

I survived the move from Richmond to Arlington, Virginia, where my classmates made jokes about how Arlington was a place where people were "dying to get in." I went through giving book reports in my below-the-Mason-Dixon-line accent until I finally talked like everyone else.

I lived the excited pangs of independence and loneliness when at the age of sixteen I went to New York City to study ballet and whatever else the city that never slept had to offer. I had been dancing since I was three and had some pretty good teachers, but NYC was the ultimate. I got into the subway circuit show of *Oklahoma!* and discovered I loved musical comedy more than ballet. When Rodgers and Hammerstein asked me to join the London company, my dad was disappointed that I wouldn't finish high school, so I turned Rodgers and Hammerstein down and went home to graduate. I've never regretted that, although I never learned much in school except how to type.

My high school was about cheerleading, football games, dancing classes, and boys. When I graduated and went back to New York, I was ready to succeed. I got into a Servel Ice Box trade show and danced accomplished pirouettes around a Servel Ice Maker. It was so boring that one night I blacked out my two front teeth for a joke and got fired. We had traveled around the country with the refrigerators on a train, so I learned about stage door johnnies who wanted their drinks straight up, never mind the ice, and could they have the pleasure of experiencing a "showgirl"? I said, "No, I'm a dancer."

After Servel I got into *Me and Juliet*, another Rodgers and Hammerstein musical, where I settled into being a Broadway gypsy and rode the subways to and from the theater because I had only enough money for lunch and dinner at the Automat, usually a peanut butter sandwich (10¢) and lemonade (lemons and sugar free at the tables). The chorus line was a family to me, but I knew I wanted to be out there singing a song and acting. The opportunity soon came when Hal Prince and Freddie Brisson came down to the basement where the chorus kids dressed and asked if any of us wanted to invest in a new musical they were putting together called *7½ Cents* (later renamed *The Pajama Game*). I said I couldn't afford an investment, but would like to audition for the show. They said fine.

A few months later I found myself dancing in front of Jerry Robbins, George Abbott (who had directed *Me and Juliet*), Hal Prince, and a strange, hunched-over little man who smoked cigarettes incessantly and paced up and down the aisles of the St. James Theatre in the dark. I remembered he was married to Joan McCracken, one of the stars of *Me and Juliet*. I also remembered him from *Kiss Me Kate* on the screen. He played the snake and a court jester. He was Bob Fosse, and our lives were to be inextricably intertwined. When Jerry Robbins pointed to me and said, "You with the legs that start at your eyeballs," I knew I was in.

Carol Haney (who danced with Bob in *Kiss Me Kate*) was the hit of *The Pajama Game* when we opened a few months later. She had no understudy, and Hal Prince asked me if I would like to try. In those days, I was dancing with a long, red ponytail whipping around my face—that is, until the stage manager dunked my head in the basement sink and said, "Cut it off. You are attracting attention away from the principals!" Hence my hairstyle, which I've never changed. So much for my sense of keeping up with fashion.

Anyway, they gave me the understudy job, but I never had a rehearsal. I had thought Carol would go on with a broken neck, so I had decided instead to understudy Gwen Verdon in *Can-Can* at the Shubert Theater down the street. Then, a few nights later, Carol sprained her ankle.

*Synchronicity was already beginning to become active in my life, as I was about to learn.*

I had my "I'm leaving" notice in my pocket when I arrived at the St. James. Across the stage door entrance stood Jerry Robbins, Bob Fosse, Hal Prince, etc. "Haney is out," they said. "You're on." I couldn't believe what I was hearing. "I'm on? *Without a rehearsal?*" I didn't know what key I sang in, I didn't know the dialogue or the lyrics, and I didn't know whether Carol's clothes would fit. I had been watching her from the wings, but performing something with your own body is another matter. Even with the aforementioned problems, all I could think of was, "I'm going to drop the hat in *Steam Heat*" (Fosse's famous hat-trick number).

I raced to Carol's dressing room. Her clothes fit me except for her shoes. I had a pair of sneakers with me from an afternoon at Jones Beach. They needed to be black. The wardrobe mistress dyed them (the black water dripped from them when I put them on). John Raitt and the conductor, Hal Hastings, wincingly went over the songs with me. With my voice, it didn't really matter what key I sang in.

There I was, waiting in the wings, when the announcer said Carol Haney would be out and I would replace her. There were "boos" from the orchestra to the second balcony. Some people threw things at the stage. The cast was lined up in the wings to observe the debacle. And I waited for the curtain to rise.

I think it was then that I realized I had an angel on my shoulder. I felt I was guided somehow. I didn't know how or by whom. But I wasn't alone. I sank into the center of my being and somehow did the show. The rest of the cast was sensitive and on their toes for any trouble I might find myself unable to handle.

I *did* drop the hat in *Steam Heat* because the spotlight blinded me. I lost it in midair, and said, "Oh shit," right out loud. The first few rows gasped and crossed their legs, but I got through the rest of it without falling into the pit. When the show was over, I took my bows with the other two *Steam Heat* dancers. The audience stood up. Buzz Miller and Peter Gennaro peeled off and left me in the center of the stage to bask in the audience's appreciation. Never had I been so lonely, but *I knew deep inside that the destiny of my life was now in alignment*. My shoulder angel smiled, and I knew I was in for a life of hard work, discipline, gratitude, and success.

I also knew somehow that I would forever be curious about those things that were "unseen" but definitely real. They were alive and well and active in my life. I would come to understand them years later.

Hal Wallis, a movie producer, had been in the audience and came backstage to ask for a meeting with me. I remembered his name from "Hal Wallis Presents Dean Martin and Jerry Lewis" (more synchronicity: the Rat Pack with Dean and Frank later).

Wallis took me to dinner, where I nearly ate the menu, too. He invited me to do a screen test with Danny Mann (the director who guided Shirley Booth and Anna Magnani to Academy Awards).

When I showed up for the screen test, Danny asked what scene I would like to do. I told him I didn't know any, and I didn't know anything about acting anyway. He asked someone for a high stool, then told me to sit on it and we just talked. I did a few steps with a long scarf and sang something quietly so he wouldn't be able to tell I couldn't sing. He smiled through it all, and I guess I did, too.

Wallis saw the test and signed me to a contract saying, "The personality test has come into being . . . no more scenes from *Voice of the Turtle*."

Somehow, what was happening to me seemed natural. It was as though it was in the flow of what was supposed to be—a kind of predetermined destiny. Dear Reader, in some metaphysical way I knew I had planned it all before I was born! I really felt that way, and at that time I didn't know what the word "reincarnation" meant. I just *knew* I had designed it before I came in.

I went on for Carol in *The Pajama Game* for about two weeks. Those weeks were a blur of learning. I rehearsed in my sleep, literally, whereupon I became aware of living on two levels of consciousness simultaneously (a state of being I employ often, by the way).

I had never been a religious person. I had gone to church a few times, and I think it said "Baptist" on my birth certificate. But at an early age I was aware of another dimension. It was invisible, but real to me. I had dreams of being guided from another place. I *knew* there was another, larger truth than what I had been taught.

When I was ten, I asked for a telescope for Christmas—a telescope and a gold cross on a chain. I used to sit out on our lawn, gaze through that telescope, and ponder on life out there. What was happening on those other stars? Were there star people who gazed down on me? I wanted to know them, feel them, ask them questions. There was never any doubt in my mind that they were there. Maybe one of them was the angel on my shoulder.

The gold cross on a chain (which I still have and treasure) was with me when I went to New York. One day I felt it missing from my neck. It was gone. At that moment I heard a voice in my head say, "Southeast corner of Fifty-seventh Street and Seventh Avenue." A voice? In my head? I took the bus to that location, got off, and there, gleaming in the sunlight, was the cross. "What's going on here?" I thought. "What . . . or who . . . is talking to me?"

My childhood seemed to have been normal. I guess I had a vivid imagination. Yet, I knew I perceived things differently than most of my friends. I was a happy-go-lucky student who wanted to be popular and smoked with boys in the backseats of cars, but subjects such as geometry and astronomy became my preferred pleasure. I felt I was remembering an acquaintance with such things. The books I read had to do with "Heroes of Civilization" who had gone out on a limb for their curiosities and beliefs. They were who I identified with—not show business people and dancers. I did have a crush on Alan Ladd until I met him and saw that he came up to my waist. And I adored Nora Kaye, who could do sixty-four fouettés and also act as well as she danced in *Fall River Legend*. When she was one of the producers of *The Turning Point*, I came to love her as a human being (more synchronicity). I told her of the time as a twelve-year-old I went backstage to see her. Because Kaye had an E on the end of her name, I thought she must be Russian and unable to understand English. Instead, she burst forth with a Brooklyn accent and invited me to sit on her lap. She remembered.

Yes, I was beginning to see the connections of synchronicity in my life, particularly the show business events. It was as though I was meant to be successful so I could contribute in other ways on a public stage when I understood them better. For example, Bob Fosse picked me out of the chorus of *Pajama Game* to sing a little part, then appointed me Carol's understudy. A few years later, Lew Wasserman, head of Universal Pictures, called me into his office (I remember his desk was completely empty and clear) and asked me what I wanted to do next. I answered, "*Sweet Charity*. And Bob Fosse should direct it." Lew said Bob was just a choreographer. I said, okay, but so was Stanley Donen. Lew agreed and sent for Fosse.

The experience with Fosse on *Charity* was magical. Of course he apologized through swirls of cigarette smoke for making us "do it a few more times." But he was brilliant, and it launched his picture career. When Bob made *All That Jazz*, he asked me to play Gwen. I told him I couldn't dance well anymore. He kept insisting, saying I was the only authentic one who could do it after all we had been through together. I said, "How can you call *All That Jazz* authentic when the leading man (you) dies at the end?" He thought a moment, and said, "If you play Gwen, I promise I'll be dead after the first preview!"

After I returned from visiting Fidel Castro in Cuba, Bob visited with me again to try to convince me to play Gwen. The pleading didn't last long. What he really wanted to know was whether I had been to bed with Fidel. I told him not only did I not sleep with the man, but when I returned to New York, my Cuban maid unpacked my bags, saw pictures of me with Fidel, and promptly quit!

Bob didn't die after the first preview of *All That Jazz*, but he did die in a more synchronistic way that made my heart turn over. He had come from a rehearsal for the revival of *Sweet Charity* and died on the street in Washington, D.C., not far from my old dancing school. My teachers watched it happen.

When I did my first one-woman show, it was Gwen who came to coach me in the rehearsal hall on the new kinds of dances. And later she played a cameo in a picture I directed called *Bruno*. We had many chats about the many sides of Fosse and what he had meant to us. I had a dream about Gwen on the night she died. She was waving at me and smiling. I believe she and Bob were in my soul group. It is said that there are twelve people in each soul group. (In numerology, twelve is the number representing the divine.) The group is composed of people we have known in other lifetimes and who facilitate each other on the soul's path of learning. Life, I was beginning to understand, is meant to enable each of us souls to learn who we are and why we act the way we do. Hopefully, by the time we leave, we've learned a little more about our fears, our happiness, and mostly, how to give love and accept it, without judgment.

Maybe that's why I love show business: We are essentially the producer, director, and star of our own comedy/drama every day, on and off the stage of life. We are all actors on our own stages, creating our own reality. The Fosse years in my life, peopled by his own actors and actresses, who overlapped mine, enabled me to accept and even revel in talented eccentricity. Fosse was an artist whose tortured soul drove him. He never believed he was good enough, funny enough, inventive enough. He never believed he could really love enough or accept love enough. He was painfully broad-stroked and honest in his assessment of himself in *All That Jazz*. He was obsessed with sex and its meaning in his life, and was threatened deeply by the recognition of the feminine in himself. Underneath, he was a kind, generous, sensitive human being who was addicted to showing the world the obsessive side of himself. Out of these complex neuroses came his great art. His dance movements turned in on themselves just as he did. Unless he was expressing sex. Then they looked like his fantasy of an orgy. The Fosse years taught me that we could use our depraved opinions of ourselves to artistic advantage.

My life in films has been basically an education in human behavior; not only in terms of acting, but also in the science of trust. The Billy Wilder/Jack Lemmon years were instructions in comedy. *Irma la Douce* and *The Apartment* were acts of pure trust on the part of Jack and me. We never had a completed script when we started, but Jack had a track record with Billy, and I was new to the equation. Billy trusted the chemistry between Jack and me, and we trusted his judgment. Frankly, I didn't know enough not to trust.

Trust is an important currency in filmmaking. Trust is required in show business as much as talent and the money to finance.

We have to trust our instincts, and we have to trust each other. That is what is meant by a "collaboration."

When I was younger, I innocently trusted nearly everyone and everything. I think I still do. I'm proud that I haven't become jaded or cynical. Instead, I've become a more sophisticated questioner. Given some of my traveling antics, I don't know how I survived. I was caught in a coup d'etat in the Himalayas (Bhutan). I got smuggled illegally into Leningrad University in the Soviet Union and had my passport stolen. I lived with the Masai in East Africa and birthed a few babies inside of a *menyatta* (village) who were named after me. I took a women's delegation to Communist China (before any other foreigners were admitted) and promptly, along with everyone else, got pneumonia. I traveled alone across the United States and took up with an Indian medicine man in Arizona, who taught me the ways of the Great Spirit while driving around in an old Dodge with $50,000 worth of turquoise jewelry he tried to sell me. Once after a trip through Romania and Czechoslovakia, I came back to Los Angeles but never returned to my house. I turned right around, went back to the airport, and flew to Mexico. I never wanted to stay in one place except to make a movie. In fact, I canceled two movies in order to trek the Santiago de Compostela Camino alone for a month, while my agent back home wondered if I'd ever work again. I went to India for a week and stayed for a month and a half. The wanderlust was an elixir for me. I always went alone and splashed up against totally foreign environments. I learned about myself. In North Africa I studied the Koran outside of mosques with friends I met. In India I studied the Bhagavad Gita while wondering if I had lived there before. Always I was in the search for this "other" truth, this "other" dimension I knew was there. Perhaps in the older, ancient cultures of foreign lands I could find a hint of something besides stardom, success, materialism, and the action of Hollywood and America. In Brazil, I had a friend with a private plane who took me to many of the psychic surgeons and healers in the Amazon. I saw that they were working with the "other" dimensions. I saw them take out human eyes to restore sight to a blind woman. One psychic surgeon removed a human heart, fixed the four-part bypass, restored it to the man's chest, and with "energy" closed the wound without stitches.

I went to Machu Picchu in Peru with a man who said he had had a love affair with an extraterrestrial. He said he was still being guided by her and could call on that guidance anytime. He proceeded to do just that. The Peruvian roads are steep, narrow, and dangerous. He took his hands off the wheel, closed his eyes and the car was "driven." I don't know by what. People don't believe me when I tell them this story. They suspect a trick of some kind, but I saw none. What was even more shocking than the invisibly driven car was the fact that it was okay with me. I trusted that what he said was true. I believe now that I never got in serious trouble or a life-threatening situation because I trusted whoever I was with. Even if some had been life-threatening, I chose to regard them as adventures. Why did I do that? Why wasn't I more left-brained suspicious about so many events? Was I totally gullible? If so, why wasn't I ever really hurt or seriously threatened? Was there really an angel on my shoulder from the beginning? And was the real lesson in life to trust that each of us has one or maybe more angels and guides? Was I talking about religion here, or was I talking about the "other"? Real spirituality did not occur to me until I was forty years old.

Now it's a few days into my chaotic move, and I'm taking a break from unpacking and am watching the 2006 midterm election returns on television. Does America have an angel on its shoulder, I wonder? Although I am a senior citizen who has happily adopted New Mexico as my home for the rest of my years, I was born in Richmond, Virginia. I was raised in the state of Virginia, responsible for eight of our presidents and through which the Mason-Dixon line, dividing the North from the South, runs.

I see now that the people of Virginia will make the decision as to whether the Democrats will control the Senate as well as the House of Representatives. I am proud of that.

Virginia was responsible for my connection to the deep meaning of the Founding Fathers and their intent for a new democracy. Virginia was why I became a political activist. Virginia was why I got deeply involved with the civil rights movement. And later my home in Arlington, Virginia, was across the Potomac River from the nation's capital, close enough for me to observe what went on in Washington, D.C., because I took the bus from Arlington every day to go to dancing school in Washington.

Now as I sit here in New Mexico watching democracy at work, I reflect on how depressed I've been in the last year about what's been going on in Washington.

I have always had an innocent, bouncy, adolescent slant on life—optimistic and maybe even naive. It has served me well, but now I'm not so sure. I always felt that everything happens just as it should—usually for the purposeful good. Now I'm feeling more deeply the need to take greater personal responsibility for what happens in this world and thinking about how I might be participating in the reality before me, not just observing it. I find myself concerned about the addiction to technology in our culture and the crippling of democracy.

To tell you the truth, I feel like democracy. I need to be helped and nurtured along so that I will retain my faith in freedom and the goodwill of people. I need to be helped down the steps of my trailer on a movie set (someone always comes to help whether I ask for it or not). I am helped in and out of cars—cars that are racing along a street that is so wired with modern technology that I wonder how the trees and birds can take it.

Now I find myself worried that the voting machines are being tampered with and that technology has swamped and crippled democracy. Technology has sometimes made my life unbearable. I can't remember my cell phone codes, my bank codes, my pin numbers, or even the phone numbers of my family and best friends because they are stuck in some other "convenient" technological contraption.

When I waited in line at United Airlines only to be told I had to check myself in via computer, I turned around and went back home. I believe Stephen Hawking is correct when he speculates that computers will surpass human intelligence soon. Technology is even making democracy obsolete because we really don't talk to each other much anymore and debate the issues of the day. Most people are on the computer. Not me. I only use a computer to read out-of-state and international newspapers and check in on my website. Nor do I use email. If someone wants to get in touch with me, I want to hear his or her voice. I want to hear the spaces between words; the hesitations when discussing something, the emotion in their voice. And more than anything I hate email computer English. No wonder newspaper reading is way down. People don't know how to read proper English anymore.

Ever since our invasion of Iraq I have been ashamed at how we Americans have mishandled ourselves, our government, and let democracy and our Founding Fathers down. My rage and futile ranting and raving within make me feel old. What happened? How did it all come to this? We have to be saved by the state that was the home of most of our Founding Fathers?

I watch the returns with a feeling of wise resignation.

My dad always teased me about being a bleeding-heart liberal who would join any cause for an underdog. "Stick to your own little row of potatoes," he would warn, but I couldn't play it safe that way. I had the blood of the Founding Fathers pounding through my heart. The pounding was accompanied by the understanding that most of our Founding Fathers had been transcendentalists. They were metaphysically and spiritually motivated. They wanted freedom from the constraints of religion in Europe. Most were Masons, some believed in reincarnation, and Jefferson even wrote his own Jeffersonian Bible, decrying how the Christian religion had been so prostituted.

Because of my patriotism and my Virginia upbringing, I was always interested in what our government was up to. I couldn't bear Richard Nixon and his lies, particularly about Vietnam, so I spent a year campaigning for George McGovern, much to the ridicule of my dad. He said McGovern had Novocaine in his upper lip and sized him up as a real loser. He said he knew Richard Nixon was a son of a bitch but that he was *our* son of a bitch. He couldn't see McGovern standing up to the Communists or understanding power in any way. I saw McGovern as a senator who didn't believe we should be in Vietnam. Bobby Kennedy once said of McGovern, "He's not the most honest senator we have, he's the *only* honest one we have."

For me, the experience of campaigning taught me about America, because I went everywhere. I made speeches in front of union hall members, chaired coffee klatches in too many living rooms to remember, did every TV show that would have me, registered voters on the street, marched in any antiwar demonstrations I could find, and turned down every movie that came my way. I was *out* where Hollywood was concerned. They thought I was crazy to give up show business in favor of McGovern. Many supporters deserted George's ship, knowing it was indeed a lost cause, but for some stalwart reason, still not completely clear to me, I stuck it out to the very end. It wasn't just blind loyalty. I couldn't live with a president who corrupted the Justice Department, the Defense Department, the Oval Office, the FBI, and CIA and who also thought he could get away with treason. That was it—I thought Richard Nixon was guilty of treason and should be impeached even before Watergate was big news.

So sitting in the living room of a hotel suite in South Dakota with McGovern and a few others, I watched the country turn on him—all but Massachusetts—the state of the assassinated ones. It was awful. It was shocking. I could picture my father's "Tsk-tsk, I told you so," back home in Virginia, totally unaware that his son of a bitch would disgrace our country and the presidency in another year. After the last soul-searing returns came in, I fled South Dakota and traveled south in a car with a friend. When we reached Texas, he said he missed the cement and action of New York and left. I continued driving. Alone.

As soon as I crossed the Texas border into New Mexico, I knew the license plates were right. "The Land of Enchantment" was enchanting. I made friends with some people and asked why there was so much white salt on the mountains above the desert.

They explained diplomatically that the white was snow. I was in heaven in high desert country. I knew then I would spend the last part of my life here. I had some things to do first, but until then I knew where I belonged. So here I sit, all these years later, above the Land of Enchantment, sageing over my life and our country and wondering if I really have the courage to go into who I *really* am. What will that journey involve?

In my home, I have what my friends call the "wall of life." It is a wall of pictures ranging from my childhood until now. I take these pictures with me if I move into a new place, and it's always fun to hang them—like pieces of a jigsaw puzzle, they fit together to cover an entire wall.

When I have people over, it's always a kick for me when they stop and stand in front of my wall of life and take it in. They see pictures of me as a young dancer, on the sets of my films, me chatting with Gorbachev, Jimmy Carter, Indira Gandhi, the Dalai Lama, George McGovern, and a prime minister or two with whom I had affairs during my "slumming in power" days. When I see photographs from my childhood, I remember that somehow I knew at the age of three in a dancing class that my life would take me around the world and back so many, many times. Dancing and show business became a springboard to everything else I wanted to accomplish in my life.

# chapter

## 2

I'M SURROUNDED BY BOXES, PICTURES, SCRIPTS, VIDEOTAPES, and all the artifacts of my wall of life. My mind-memory flicks back and forth, up and down, in and out of events. Now I can see more clearly how the people and events in my life were inexorably connected. It takes years to come to that understanding. My show business movie years were cemented to my political and traveling years. The people I chose to love and have as friends were educators in each of those adventures. I couldn't know the world inside of myself unless I knew more of the world outside, and the more I understood the world outside, the more I felt I had been there before. A kind of comforting familiarity enveloped me even when I was in trouble in a foreign land. What an entertainment it is to relive my past from a present-day perspective. It's the same as approaching a scene in a movie. There are so many ways to play the same words, the same actions, the same characters. Perspective is everything. I can see now that my perspective is what I choose it to be, regardless of what occurred in the past.

My mind flashes to examples: the day—I must have been sixteen—that I returned from dance class to tell my parents I had lost the role of Cinderella because I was too tall and gawky. I tried to dash up the stairs to avoid their reaction, but my father stopped me with a tirade. "What makes you think you could really dance anyway? You shouldn't expect so much of yourself. And yet you say you want to be in musical comedy—well, you know you can't sing or act, why don't you look at reality? Then you won't be so devastated if you already know the truth." I tripped and fell from his words. I became so hysterical I vomited. He didn't stop. "Don't dare," he admonished. "Don't dare. You will be hurt if you do." I climbed the rest of the stairs, leaving my vomit for him to clean up. Mother remained silent.

Now I realize Dad was talking about himself. He had been taught by his parents not to dare. So he didn't. In effect, though, he was teaching me to do just that—I would not only dare in my life, I would fulfill the dreams he never allowed himself to fulfill. I would do it all for him—not only for him—for both of them. They had both felt subdued and smothered by the trials and tribulations of child raising when in truth what they really wanted was to be free. That's my perspective, perhaps theirs would be different. Of course they enjoyed raising a family and everything that entailed, but I believe that their thwarting their own personal expressive desires caused my brother and me to use them as a negative example and taught us to choose otherwise. At the same time that I did indeed receive love and caring, I received cues to avoid the same stifling life for myself. I saw what it could do to the soul. Therefore, I became a freewheeling wanderer who was never particularly interested in set-tling down to a "normal" married, child-raising life, even if I *could* work and express myself at the same time.

I am everlastingly grateful to my mom and dad for being part of the contract that I believe we had with each other. I chose them and they chose me. The scene on the stairs is a part of my movie that I will never forget.

Another scene comes to mind. I was running a relay in a track meet in high school. Dad had come to see it. When the relayer handed me the stick, I dropped it. I dropped the stick. Never have I been so ashamed, humiliated, or full of self-loathing—before or since. No ill-received film or bad, humiliating opinion of me has had the effect of my dropping that stick. I was the reason we lost the race, and it happened in front of my "Don't Dare" father. Who was he to me? Who had he been before? Was he the male authority figure I always wanted to please, which would serve me well with male authority figure directors on a movie set in Hollywood years later? It has often been said that actors, and particularly actresses, fall in love with their directors because, of course, they are our father figures.

I've noticed in my advancing years that I have become a "crone" in Hollywood, which exacts a kind of impatient respect from most people. They either respect me for what I've done or would prefer to see me as "invisible" so that they don't have to contend with what I'm about. I'm very aware these days of how deeply debilitating being "invisible" can be.

In fact, I'm going to do a picture called *Poor Things,* which was inspired by the story of two older women who, frustrated with being invisible, endeavor, according to police, to exact their revenge with the following plot: They visit homeless shelters, take out insurance policies on certain individuals, make themselves the beneficiaries, then run over the *Poor Things* with their van and kill them. Since they were so "invisible" no one noticed for a long time. (They are now awaiting trial in Los Angeles.) I think it's hilarious, and I admit I'd probably benefit from some therapy in determining just why I find such dark-sided humor so funny. When I tell people the characters and plot, they all say I'm perfect for the part. What do they mean?

It's also very funny to me that people sometimes get tongue-tied when meeting and talking to me. First of all, they sometimes think I can see right through them (which *is* happening more and more). But they also often think I talk to spiritual entities who inform me of their futures, and they don't want to be seen. So rather than making me invisible, they'd prefer to be invisible around me . . . fascinating.

However, with values crumbling in our world, and religious conflict over God causing most of the world wars, most of my Hollywood friends are beginning to see more metaphysical spiritual connections in their lives and work. It doesn't seem to prevent them, however, from making money on the screen with horror, violence, perverted sex, and so on, but at least now most of them sigh in self-deprecating defense that that's what the public wants. The grosses seem to bear them out. But at least many of them now have the good grace to be ashamed around the watercooler that they had to resort to such material.

As a Scotch-Irish person where money is concerned (I have deep pockets and short arms), I personally find it appalling that people of extraordinary means need to look for ways to spend more money. They purposely desire more expensive homes and cars that they don't need and can't use. These same people call themselves spiritual.

I made a decision sometime ago that I wouldn't do a violent special effects movie just because it would be a big grosser.

I believe that the values we play in will return to us in kind. The laws of karma are at work even in Hollywood. What we put out to the public will come back to us.

I'm sad that character-driven movies, which are, after all, about us, have been regulated to a category called "women's films" or "specialty films." It's difficult to raise money for such films, yet they are usually the ones that win the awards if they are good.

To raise money for a metaphysically spiritual film is almost impossible, because the studio heads say they need to put fear-inducing material on the screen because there is so much real fear in our culture that audiences prefer to go into denial about. They'd rather feel "fantasy-fear" with their entertainment so they don't have to face real fear in their lives.

To do a horror film for the sake of horror is anathema to me. To promulgate fear regarding extraterrestrials is also a crime to me, yet that's what makes money and gets ratings. It is dispiriting and a denial of what could possibly be help from other than Earth people for our survival. More on that later.

As I put up my "wall of life" pictures, I'm reminded once again how privileged I have been to work with the finest talents Hollywood ever called its own. I witnessed their personal and working habits. It was always an entertainment to observe closely those whose entire lives were dedicated to entertaining. When I worked with Wilder, Lemmon, and other stars and directors in my life, we never talked about spiritual or metaphysical subjects. Sometimes I would try to initiate a conversation, but they shied away in embarrassment and sometimes fear. Billy Wilder spoke freely of his time in Germany and his trek to America, where he became more conversant with our sports and trends than we were. Jack Lemmon was a haunted man

who battled his demons with alcohol all his adult life, but recognizing any sort of spirituality never seemed to occur to him. Jack Nich-
olson was a wonder of free association. He required complete focus
to understand the point of his associations—sounding maddeningly
brilliant, by the way, even though it was hard to discern what he was
talking about. And when he exhibited his own violence, you knew
it was coming from a truly dangerous place. He seemed to want to
use the violence in his colorful characters rather than assuage it in
his own life. I remember a conversation I had with Norman Mailer
once, who claimed neurosis was necessary to a real artist. He might
be right, I don't know. I've tried to make my neuroses work for
me . . . such as absolute discipline, no small talk, telling the truth as
I see it regardless, really neurotic anger at injustice, and deep fury
at presidents who abuse the public trust . . .

The early Dean and Jerry were a study in competition. Dean
was the funny one—Jerry was funny but mathematical. I worked
with them when they were breaking up—it wasn't pretty. Dean
was not happy with Jerry's obsessive control over him and the pro-
duction. Jerry needed to be the center of stardom. I experienced it
one day when I did a song and dance number with him on a stair-
way in the movie *Artists and Models*. The number was constructed
so that the girl (me) was the funny one. Jerry couldn't bear it. He
went to his trailer and sulked until Hal Wallis, the producer, came
to the set and threatened him with lawsuits. I, of course, being a
dancer, thought I had done something wrong, and no one was
telling me. We resolved all our problems, but I remember feeling
so sorry for Jerry's insecurities when he was so brilliant.

Dean was not so forgiving and in the film immediately after
*Artists and Models*, he just walked out of a script meeting and
was gone from Jerry's life for twenty years until they did a benefit

together. There was no contact between him and Jerry. Dean simply never looked back and went on to team up with Frank Sinatra frequently.

It was interesting for me to watch the two Italians who had "mob" beginnings originally fashion "dangerous" public personas for themselves, which worked so well in Vegas that you couldn't get a table either to gamble or to see a show. Dean, by the way, was a blackjack dealer the night Bugsy Segal opened the Flamingo. He was the real deal, while I always had the impression that Frank was a pretender to the mafia throne. I used to hear Giancana and Fraschetti talk about Frank as "The Singer." Dean was the one who told them to fuck themselves whenever he was summoned.

When I did the original *Ocean's Eleven*, of course, we didn't know it would go to *Ocean's Thirteen*. Those days are dreamily blurry to me, and I perceive them in an entirely different way now. Of one thing I am sure: The public loves to fantasize about good-looking, dangerous teams of men.

Dean and Frank were my buddies. I was referred to as their mascot. That's true, I suppose, but from the vantage point of being a senior citizen, I realize what an adolescent caper it all was. The Rat Pack will never come this way again. We threw caution to the winds, sprinkled with an underlying acceptance that higher forces ran the world (mafia and government). Certainly I met and even socialized with the prevailing leaders of the underworld, but what struck me was how impressed they were with my absence of fear. I can't say I didn't know who they were, but that knowledge meant nothing to me. Nothing they did or said really frightened me. I don't know why.

That was laughable to Dean and Frank. They even teased me about it when I'd pull a water pistol out and point it at Sam Giancana, who immediately went for the .45 in his vest holster. They'd laugh. I don't know why I did these things. Some kind of small-town bravado, I suppose, but they seemed to listen to me when I complained about their intimidation of another person at the dinner table. I remember telling Sam to go fuck himself when he tried to get me to eat his spaghetti, and I was trying to lose weight. When he grabbed my arm, I kneed him in the balls. Sammy Davis stopped that skirmish and shoved me out of the room, but not before I told Sam to go fuck himself one more time.

Later, when I did my club act, I noticed that many guys with their pinkie rings gave me the high sign from front-row tables in Vegas. What was fear anyway? Wasn't it a game? Isn't that what the world revolves around? It's all perception and what we choose to be afraid of.

I've since become close friends with Sam Giancana's former girlfriend Phyllis McGuire and some serious members of the mob. I've learned what they really thought of Frank (a singer) and Dean (the real McCoy). Where I'm concerned, they say I knew how to keep my mouth shut, and I'm "fun." Wow. They are the only humans on the planet who think I keep my mouth shut.

I hung out for many years with Dean and Frank and did many movies with them. They knew nothing of my metaphysical musings, but later on in Frank's life he told me he believed he had lived before and would live again. He was a deep-thinking man who longed to control secrets. Dean was ashamed of his lack of education. In fact, during parties at his own home he would retire to his den and watch reruns of *Kojak* rather than risk a serious conversation. His best friend and agent was my agent, Mort Viner. Mort and Dean lived together on and off, keeping each other company for many years. When Dean died, a light went out in Mort's life. He took care of the estate, Dean's children, Dean's music, and many of Dean's women, but he no longer had his buddy.

I never had a physical relationship with any one of the group. People (including Kitty Kelley) don't believe that, but it's true. I had a small crush on Dean, but it never went anywhere. I was too young, and Jeannie (his wife) was always around. That didn't stop me from being with other married men, usually my leading men, who, in our business, usually make it a point to know their attractive leading ladies intimately for the duration of the film, whether there was a wife and kids at home or not. It was understood that we were working and expressing ourselves in a fantasy world where it would be over when the location was complete. The women did the same thing. It was accepted, however painfully, that doing love scenes during the day didn't cease at wrap.

One of the more fascinating metaphysical nonrelationships I ever had was with Peter Sellers. Peter was a well-known believer in esoteric traditions. He believed he had lived before, which was the basis for his genius in playing various characters. He also had visited a numerologist, who told him his numbers did not fit with his wife's. He proceeded to divorce her. When we did *Being There* together, Peter would never have lunch or dinner with me. One Valentine's Day on the set I received five dozen roses. I knew they were from Peter, so I couldn't understand why he denied my thank-yous. Soon after the film wrapped, I was asked by several people how I enjoyed my affair with Peter. I was thrown. They went on to tell me they had heard him on the phone with me doing love-sex talk. I couldn't process what I was being told because he wouldn't socialize with me at all. Then I realized he was having a fantasy during *Being There* that we were the two characters in the script. If he had had dinner with me, it would have broken the fantasy. *What a complicated spell we weave, when the characters we do believe.*

Lord Richard Attenborough and I worked together on *The Bliss of Mrs. Blossom* in 1968. We played husband and wife. His daughter played with my daughter during the shoot. It was a delightful experience. Between takes he would tell me of his plans to direct a picture based on the life of Gandhi, the Indian prime minister. He wanted me to play the reporter, Margaret Bourke-White, because I had spent a lot of time in India. I said yes and waited . . . and waited. The years passed. And as has been the case several times in my life, I got too old. I was supposed to play Roxie in *Chicago,* too, but because of script problems there was a delay . . . then another script when I was ready to play Velma. More script problems. Finally, with the latest script, I was right for the lesbian warden. I said no and thought the movie was one of the best ever made. Fosse would have been so proud that the musical he devised as a gift to Gwen so she wouldn't divorce him won an Oscar and kept his talent and name alive.

Anyway, back to Lord Richard. A couple of years ago, Dickie (that's what we call him) had another script he wanted to do. It was based on a true story called *Closing the Ring,* about a woman who was loved by three men who hung out together with her during adolescence. It spans some fifty years and due to circumstances involving the deaths of two of them, she ends up marrying all three. He planned to make the picture partly in Ireland and my preoccupation was how I would get my beloved dog Terry into the United Kingdom. Each time he thought he had the financing in place, my obsession reared its head again. I even wrote a book called *Out on a Leash,* which revolved around my fear that I would have to be away from Terry if the picture did happen. In fact, something worse happened. Dickie lost his daughter and grand-daughter in the tsunami in Indonesia, which made my problem less than insignificant. He plowed forward, though, and finally raised the money from the Film Commissions of Canada, Ireland, and the United Kingdom, which meant we would have to shoot in Canada and Ireland.

Because of Attenborough and his movie, I learned that Terry and I could get along without each other. I also learned under his direction that underplaying can be masterful if I trust it. Even at eighty-three, he never missed a nuance or a thought pattern that crossed an actor's mind. He is truly a master of his medium. But more important than the movie was the renewed relationship he and I and his wife Sheila developed, revolving around the death of his daughter and granddaughter. I think some of my spiritual understanding regarding why people, regardless of age, choose to leave helped them a little. We talked for long hours at dinner every night about the deeper meaning of those things that sting and devastate us. Dickie had always been a music devotee because it moved him so much. Since his daughter's passing, he said he hasn't allowed a note of music to cross his ears. Otherwise, he would break down and fall apart. The picture we made together is basically about a woman who won't allow herself to grieve. Perhaps he was living through my performance and could now allow himself a release. Watching Dickie's eighty-three-year-old lifestyle will be a lesson for me when I finally reach that age.

He has a ritualistic approach to all activities. For example, at dinner he lowers himself into his seat at the table with a grand and royal style. He shakes out his napkin with a flourish and beckons the waiter with a gentle command. No conversation ensues prior to his inquiry as to what "starters" are on for the night. He engages, with much speculation, a discussion as to what would be best with the wine he prefers, and of course, the entrée. He will briskly butter a roll while waiting for what he orders, but won't eat much of it. Attenborough is a diabetic, which, of course, rules his epicurean tastes. He hasn't had sugar for forty years and said more than anything else he longed for chocolate. I sent for a big box of sugar-free chocolates from Señor Murphy in Santa Fe, and the first night he ate eleven pieces!

When he eats his entrée, he precisely cuts his meat or fish like a surgeon and washes it down with a wine he's chosen as though it's a precious elixir. His movements are deliberate and rather like slow motion. He's in no hurry anymore. He knows the food will be there, and there's no need to rush. It's conversation that is important. He doesn't like distractions. His dessert is fruit or none at all, and he is careful not to lower his eyes jealously over someone else's chocolate cake. When he is finished, he politely wipes his lips, pushes his chair from the table, ceremoniously says good night, and strides up to bed. He will sleep from midnight to six the next morning. He has laid out his next day's wardrobe according to the projected weather and is never late on the set. He is there hours before the rest of us to set up the shots. I don't know what he has for breakfast because I'm never there that early. He allows the actors to play the scene the way we want, and then like a wise but displeased professor, makes suggestions that improve everyone's performance a hundredfold. I saw actors (including myself) play a scene as though we were amateurs, and one or two suggestions from Attenborough, and we looked like genuine pros. He often said he couldn't understand how any director could direct if he hadn't acted himself. His direction has to do with how your face is experiencing the meaning of the words themselves. "Lift your head into the light, we'll see what you mean more." "Don't move your arm when you say that line, it detracts from the drama of the line." "Don't let us see tears, the audience will be more moved by your attempt to control them."

He made the atmosphere on the set completely comfortable and free, which led to most of us becoming out-of-control children with our opinions and high-strung laughter. If truth be told, we actors are basically children longing to express ourselves in any way. Say one mean sentence with real vitriol, and we shrivel back into our childhoods, which never gave us enough love and attention in the first place. You can depend on really fine actors never having had enough love. It's an occupational prerequisite. Show me an actor who had enough love in childhood, and I'll show you someone who should be a cruise director taking care of organizing others on vacation.

At lunchtime, Dickie would sleep for forty-five minutes and eat for fifteen. He could sleep anywhere—in his chair, his trailer, under the camera, his car, or even standing up as long as one of the grips propped him up. He got the flu on the picture and worked every day in the rain. Nothing or no one could make him rest or go to bed. He said if he did rest, his time would be over. He has no plans for retirement because that would be the death of him. His next picture is *Tom Paine,* the story of the great American patriot whose pamphlets, *Common Sense* and *Age of Reason* sparked the American Revolution. The script is by Trevor Griffiths, and the budget is around $100,000,000. I believe he will make it if he can find the financing.

I mention the Attenborough relationship in my life because of its own synchronicity. He was instrumental regarding my fear

of being away from my baby dog; I was able to help him understand in small part the death of his daughter and granddaughter.
I observed the need for ritual in old age, I learned how gentle,
strong, and articulate direction can change a performance. I realized how necessary grieving can be, and I needed to understand
that not all English people are diplomatic pains in the butt. I think
our picture is excellent and worth all the synchronistic lessons.
Last, but not least, I learned from an acting point of view that
subtlety can be masterful, not boring.

My wall of life is beginning to take shape. I have photographs
from every picture I've done. There is the ensemble photo of all of
us from *Steel Magnolias*. To me, *Steel Magnolias* represented the
power of the female. Even Herb Ross, the director, was floored
by it. Herb was a talented but often pompous man who had come
from being a tall, gangly, flat-footed gypsy in the dance world in
New York, to marrying the prima ballerina assoluta Nora Kaye.
When Nora died, he married Lee Radziwill and became part of
the Kennedy family, so to speak.

Before shooting in Natchitoches, Louisiana, Herb took the
art director to the location and promptly ordered him to redeco-
rate the rented house he and Lee would be living in. Herb was
very involved with self-presentation. He could be a really nice
man, but often quite cutting to others, particularly after Nora
died. In front of the crew he advised Dolly Parton to take some
acting lessons. He ridiculed Julia Roberts into tears. "You are
wasting the older, more experienced actors' time, Julia," he would
say as he demanded Scene 23 to be done again. But we women
stuck together, literally. We would surround whichever actress was
being humiliated and stare him down. That usually worked. One

day I was trying to help the focus puller by showing him my moves so he could focus. Herb saw me and began a tirade. "How dare you tell the focus puller where you'll be moving; *I'm* directing this picture." I was shocked, as was everyone. So I thought it was time for me to step up. I knew him better and longer than the others, from our days in New York and *The Turning Point*. I asked him to come sit by me for a minute. He did. I explained that ever since Nora died he was becoming a bitch, and it was not respectful to her or to us. He looked at me like someone had finally told him the truth. He paused for a moment and said, "You're right. Thank you for challenging me. I'll do better." And he did. I will always remember his willingness to look at his behavior. I've wondered how it felt for him to be scorned by Julia Roberts when in her next film she became the biggest star in the world . . . karma in play.

Years later, Herb and Lee divorced acrimoniously. When I heard he was in the hospital with depression, I called him. But he wouldn't talk to anyone. He lay in bed, silent, and in psychic pain. I lamented what happened to him. Such success and talent in Hollywood was all so . . . transitory. The beautiful house, filled with antiques and sophistication, hosted many a great Hollywood party. His stentorian tone of pomposity often motivated Nora to say, "Oh, Herbert, you are so full of shit—come off it, for fuck's sake!" (My twelve-year-old Russian role model who didn't speak English!)

As I look back at the photos of my time in Tinseltown, I realize that everything is different now. The era of Hollywood parties with flaming entrées served by gentlemen in white gloves and tuxedos is a past dream, replaced by buffets of health food grabbed on the run before a screening. The studio system, which alternately ruled and protected us, is gone. Now if you are caught driving drunk or smoking dope, you're on your own. You plan and scheme your own career and decision-making progress. You want to make a film from a good piece of material, you make the calls yourself. One thing remains true. The business is about relationships—always has been and always will be. If your name is mud because of behavioral problems, people don't want to work with you. If you're mean but make money, they just wait for your first flop—gleefully. Everyone feels better if big people flop, it makes the little people less self-conscious about their own lack of success: Success is the name of it all. How meaningless it really is, though. As long as you've made enough money to pay your mortgage and for a night out on the weekend with someone you love, I say, relax, do what you want as long as you love it.

Mike Nichols is an example of sensitivity and knowing what and whom he loves. A consummate artist who is relaxed with his years and says, "I'm sitting here in front of my crackling fire, waiting for my wife to come home from work." No competition. On the contrary—admiration. When he waited a whole day for the set of one of the numbers in *Postcards from the Edge* to be painted, he was calm, non-self-indulgent, and commanding. He knew the brown walls were depressing. They, in his mind, ruined the gaiety of the scene. Who knows? He couldn't do it in all good conscience without a change of color.

Meryl Streep seems to have exquisitely integrated her role-playing in her life. She is, in my opinion, the best we have, even if sometimes you can see her acting. Her understanding of illusion and reality is her underlying tool. When I admired her work in *Cry in the Dark*, where she played a mother whose child had been kidnapped by a dingo, her scene on the witness stand particularly caught my attention. "Did you *become* the dingo during that scene?" I asked. "Yes." She smiled. "I'm so glad you saw that." Who else would have thought of acting a dingo in order to prove her innocence as a mother?

During the last few years I became aware that I was acting in films that had already been filmed. I was playing a Mrs. Robinson in *Rumor Has It* that had been done magnificently by Anne Bancroft in *The Graduate*. Was I to do an illusion within an illusion? I felt all right about playing Mrs. Robinson because our writer, Ted Griffin, knew the real Mrs. R. and wrote her accordingly. The experience on that film was not so much about making a movie as it was about witnessing Ted get fired as the director and Jennifer Aniston go through having her life raked over the coals of hell by the media. She was a real, live, hurt person whose life and troubles were achingly real to her while the tabloids made up their own reality. Why has celebrity gossip become so commercial? Is it because the lives of "real people" have become so mundane and desperate to themselves that they need to see celebrities go through hell to feel better? That's how Hollywood feels about its own. The other guy should fail so I'll feel better. "High water lifts all boats" has become a forgotten concept.

I watched Jennifer struggle with whether to use her own pain in her character or whether to construct more discipline around her talent and resort to technique. I don't know what I would have done . . . probably the latter, because if you use your personal pain to portray a character in pain, you can lose your way and maybe even get out of character. In any case, "reality and reel-ality" were occurring before my eyes, and I wondered if she would ever allow herself to grieve when she was expected to be a consummate professional in public.

The lives of famous people are teaching exercises for the public. And in turn we learn from the public in accordance with how they respond to us. Everyone's life is a movie—on and off the screen. We act in relation to how we perceive ourselves and how we are perceived. Perception then becomes the reality, and everyone's perception is different. Where is the center of reality? Wherever *we* are.

*Bewitched* was a painful experience for me. Again, I was playing a beloved character that had already been done. The characters in the TV series were what was so enjoyable, but "marketing" at the studio decided to go with the love story. The audience didn't respond. Nicole Kidman is an actress of exquisite range whose Dresden china beauty is breathtaking. She has extraordinary focus and can act anything. She is so otherworldly that I took to calling her my "alien." She didn't seem to mind. She was so charmingly diplomatic in her closed "I will not discuss my divorce from Tom" way that she could give any government lessons. I watched in incredulity as she glided through the picture with no temperament, working impossibly long hours and looking like an angel at six in the morning after having slept only four hours. She did photo shoots on the weekends and shot commercials in Paris for Chanel, returning to work Monday perfectly fresh, with not a word about where she had been.

Nicole is an ethereal being who captured my imagination as to who she really is. I think she, like Meryl, periodically needs to be other people for her mental health and identity. They literally transform themselves as they inhabit their own studied and well-thought-out illusions. I wondered if these geniuses would be lost if suddenly there were no more characters for them to become.

Acting is the ultimate imaginative metaphysical art form. How do you really know what is real or not? That must be the intriguing mystery for the audience. Did we really fall in love with our costar? Was that real blood? Are those real tears? Is she really a bitch, and is he as sexy as he seems?

The world of art and expression will live so much longer than politics because it preserves our imagination against time. I look at my life as an expression of my questions and convictions, and now I see that each step of learning along the way has been the enactment of synchronicity . . . even moving into a new house.

# chapter

# 3

THE FIRST TIME I WALKED INTO WHAT WOULD BECOME MY new house, I knew I wanted to live in it. The front door opened to a spectacular eagle's-nest view of the surrounding mountains and the valley below. But something even more startling struck me. I suddenly had a feeling about the previous owner. I asked the house sitter if a dancer had lived in it, and if she had died at the top of the stairs (stairs I hadn't even seen yet). The house sitter didn't know if the former owner, an elderly woman she knew only as "Brigitta," had been a dancer, and she certainly didn't know where or how she had died. I saw the rest of the house in my head before I walked around it. Then I met the real estate agent at a coffee shop and bought the house fifteen minutes later. "Brigitta" turned out to be Vera Zorina, a ballet dancer in Hollywood whom I had greatly admired (and who was also George Balanchine's second wife) and yes, she had called out to her husband from the top of the stairs to say good-bye before she died. The fact that I would be able to live in the home of a dancer like Vera Zorina struck me as a wonderful example of synchronicity. Whenever I become aware of synchronicity in my life, I feel I have been given a gift. A gift we all have, by the way, if we would just acknowledge it. Frank Joseph helped me understand the nature of synchronicity in his books, and I thank him for his research.

The term "synchronicity" was coined by one of the twentieth century's most influential thinkers, the Swiss psychologist Carl Jung. Jung defined synchronicity as "any apparent coincidence that inspires a sense of wonder and personal meaning or particular significance in the observer. It is a perceived connection between two or more objects or events or persons without any recognizable cause." He used the term for the first time in 1930 to describe a situation in which apparently unrelated events converged to form a shared experience regarded as momentous by the person or persons experiencing it. As an example of synchronicity, for no apparent reason you suddenly remember a friend you have not thought of or heard from in years, and just then the telephone rings and the voice on the other end belongs to that person. Did you experience mental telepathy? Or was it something else, something deeper, something grander, something even more inexplicable? These events can range from apparently minor incidents to those that have a profound impact on your life, including those that are life-transforming or even lifesaving. These synchronistic events occur more frequently than we realize. But I don't think it can be called coincidence; I don't think it can be called accident. I think we are experiencing something that is not a new phenomenon, but we are beginning to realize that we're connecting with the very essence of primordial life itself, and maybe to the roots of what I would call timeless consciousness.

Synchronistic events, to me, point toward an organizational principle of the universe and suggest that our connection with a higher order of consciousness is never far from the surface of ordinary awareness. In one sense synchronicity can be called a meaningful intersection of paths. And in another as an interface with an alternative dimension of reality. There is a kind of connecting principle between people and events. Maybe they are a bridge for communication with the creative source for our universe. When it happens to you, you examine your feelings. You experience a sense of awe and mystery. The experience stirs up, through some type of deep resonance, a feeling of truth, some kind of intuitive knowingness. You feel less alone, as if touched by a mysterious and hidden cocreative partner. Could that partner be the God Source? Did the experience generate a high motivation and energy? Did it even make you experience passion? By recognizing these synchronistic events, we have a new purpose and meaning for our life because we are living and working with Creation. If we listen to these events, to these occurrences, we can develop and enhance our creativity or our cocreativity for serving all of life, and then we develop a passion for all living things and for our environment. Synchronistic events can be seen as little miracles through which this unseen but powerful consciousness manifests itself into our lives. We still have our free will. That is, we have the choice to ignore these little events, we can even ridicule them, but we would be ignoring our inner partner, our inner source of help that's like an artful mosaic. And by being open to that inner partner, we soon discover our unique role within the larger design of life and our destiny.

For example, you might find yourself broke at one time, desiring to buy something that you are not able to afford, and suddenly you find money hidden in a drawer that is exactly the amount of money you need to buy what you want. You might find, as I have experienced lately in this world of technological communication, that I wanted to know something about a certain subject. I would turn on the television set and there is that subject being discussed in depth on the History Channel. These events happen to millions of people every day. Sometimes we ignore them, sometimes we explore the depth and breadth of what they mean. I don't think it is a question of luck. *Synchronicity is the connecting link that we have to a nonmaterial and nonphysical reality*. It may be beyond our physical and mental understanding, but it is there nevertheless. It can't be explained as accident or coincidence. Proof of its existence has been investigated by many philosophies and religions that have suspected or affirmed it for thousands of years.

Meaningful synchronicities happen to everyone. Whether one is aware of them is the question. And the person who is aware of the occurrence is by far the best qualified to define and understand and comprehend it, because it is personal, reassuring that person that there is a great and caring intelligence helping his or her destiny.

Obviously, then, appreciating the synchronicity of these events in your life gives you a deepened sense of identity and self-worth, while it also gives meaning and direction and purpose to your existence. In its highest manifestation, synchronicity is nothing less than your personal connection to the ultimate mystery of the source in the universe. Sometimes they are the most important episodes in your life, incidents that quite literally transform you. In time, these synchronistic events, if you really pay attention to them, can lead to profound self-discoveries about who you really are and what you really are here for.

The Rigveda, one of the four ancient Hindu sacred texts, was written more than 3,500 years ago, and in its writing it describes unexpectedly up-to-date information that was as meaningful in ancient India as it is today. It was written by an unknown author long before scientists could have been capable of understanding the following words: "There is an endless net of threads throughout the universe, the horizontal threads are in space, the vertical threads are in time. At every crossing of the threads there is an individual, and every individual is a crystal bead. The great light of the Absolute Being illuminates and penetrates every crystal bead, and every crystal bead reflects, not only the light from every other crystal in the net, but also every other reflection throughout the entire universe." This sounds like today's quantum mechanics, which states that creation is a vast web of interrelated realities, that invisible spiritual bonds connect every detail of the universe.

As long ago as the Enlightenment, the Renaissance, and the Middle Ages, even back during classical civilization, and before that, in the Bronze Age, perhaps even in prehistory, these invisible spiritual bonds preoccupied the minds of human beings. The invisible spiritual bonds of synchronicity could *not* be dismissed as superstition, because it was so seriously being investigated by many of the world's greatest thinkers, then and now.

The problem seems to be this: Synchronicity seems irrational and illogical, and it defies clinical examination. But perhaps the real truth is irrational from our mechanical and materialistic point of view. When you begin to become aware of the synchronicity of the events in your life, your life takes on a truly magical quality that has nothing to do with logic. The right person, the right place, the right time enters your life at a strategic moment, which seems blindingly without logical motivation. These synchronistic events have happened to me often. For example, when I got lost on the Santiago de Compostelo Camino for nearly three days, my parents seemed to come together in my head and guided me back to the correct path. Many times people I long to hear from will call me at the moment I am thinking of them. Things I wanted to understand will come from overhearing someone else's conversation, which I feel was meant for me.

I even believe that George W. Bush is our president for synchronistic reasons, as much as I hate to see it. He has certainly forced us as individuals to take more responsibility for the actions of our government. He is a negative synchronistic teacher who is making each of us accountable for what we do or *don't* do in our system of responsible, free democracy. Perhaps Al Gore was synchronistically meant to win an Oscar and even a Nobel Peace Prize nomination instead of the presidency. As a child, I was always interested in star beings, and here I end up in the backyard of sightings . . . New Mexico. And I believe I was synchronistically meant to live in an ex-dancer's house in order to keep my beginnings as a dancer alive and with me always as I walk the trails around the house for my senior citizen exercise!

When I learned to respect these events and live my life by being aware of the synchronicity of them, I saw that they had been there for me all the time if I had just noticed them. Then I had to decide what they meant. I took what they call a "leap of faith." It was difficult at first to trust my life to this unseen power, but when I finally surrendered to it, my life became profoundly magical. The more I acted on my feelings and my intuitions, the more reliable the power became. If I accepted that the meaningful coincidences were messages and instructions, advice, warnings, and guidance to me from the unseen God Source of my intuitive inner self, where the ultimate truth of my identity sat, then I realized that the information given to me must be truthful and for my benefit, because it was coming from an all-loving source. I then began to lead a more authentic life, and I began to become more and more aware of my own personal truth. All I really did was surrender. The power of surrender was so much more powerful and meaningful than my will. When I didn't know how to play a scene, I simply surrendered to the "unseen," and it came to me. When I didn't know what was going wrong with a relationship, I surrendered until it became blindingly clear. I even used "surrender" to direct me during rush hour for the best direction to go to avoid traffic.

The power of surrender to a guided synchronicity has been the most meaningful lesson of my life. I wish it hadn't taken so long!

Synchronicities that happen to us are like fingerprints. Everyone has them, and every individual possesses a unique set of fingerprints. If you keep a close record of your own personal coincidences over time, you will begin to experience the revelation of yourself in relation to the unseen God Source. Once, various mystery religions revered them as messages from the gods and were believed to possess the expertise necessary for decoding them. The ancient mysteries were teachings about the relationship between man and Creation, principles considered too esoteric and sacred for public consumption and imparted only to students in a series of revealing initiations. When these cults were outlawed and aggressively suppressed by successive Christian emperors, their secrets vanished with them.

There are many types of synchronicity. There can be synchronicity in numbers that seem to pop up in your life—in a hotel room you're living in, in the telephone numbers that you are given, in your license plates, in your tax returns. That would lead us to the subject of numerology and what numbers mean in the course of human lives. But you have to exert your free will and investigate what the numbers mean to you.

There can be environmental synchronicity, as in lightning storms during a funeral, the sudden appearance of a cloud when you are most depressed, thunder at the moment you say something profound. Some people will see a very bright meteor when they have a brilliant thought or creative idea. There are people who are synchronistically sensitive to geological phenomena relating to earthquakes and thundershowers or other celestial occurrences. I have come to learn that this awareness provides a link between our subconscious minds and nature. This might not be as unusual as we think, since our very bodies are composed of zinc and copper and iron and salt water and potassium—all elements of the Earth. So the electrical impulses of our subconscious brains sometimes resemble the flashes of lightning. Our physical relationship with the planet and the elements is therefore close and deep. It would seem logical to conclude that our total existence is woven into the very fabric of nature, so much so that we have the capacity to feel its nuance in the same way we experience the physical reality of our own bodies. The Native American historian who senses geological upheaval is able to do so because his subconscious mind and the Earth's subterranean mind stand in the same relation to each other as do his physical body and the natural world. They are so intertwined that earthquakes and his physical unease are one in the same sensation. If we accept that there is an organic, profoundly personal link between individual human beings and the natural world, we can experience a feeling of awe and wonder for our own identity and its cosmic significance.

Many people have synchronicity with animals. To the human being, animals are archetypes, powerful symbols representing our instinctual relationship to the world. Synchronicity involving animals is perhaps the most frequent and ancient of all. There are many examples in history of birds being instrumental in helping and guiding human leaders. We know that the eagle guided Napoleon in all of his pursuits. The owl seems to be the soul's transformation through the dissolution of physical form. The swan is something of a death symbol in its archetype, but its emphasis is more on spiritual transition than death. I experienced that myself when my mother passed. Two swans appeared on the lake just outside the house where I was living, and I was sure they had some relationship to my mother as I gazed out the window. Some hours later, I learned that she had passed. In Greek mythology, the sun god's chariot is pulled across the night sky by a swan. A wolf was regarded as the ruler of the dead or the other world. In Native American tradition, a wolf is associated with the moon or the psychic side of life and is known as the teacher. Dogs, of course, being familiar to all of us, provide countless stories of their uncanny synchronistic behavior and interaction with their human companions. I have heard many stories of dogs saving their owners' lives, of warning them against danger. I had an experience where my little dog Terry did not want me to go on a trip. I got the feeling from her, I decided not to go, and I learned later something happened to the airplane. The household cat personifies grace and the ability to pass softly between opposing forces using the art of serene balance. The puma, the lion, the tiger, the cheetah, and the panther are variations of the themes of leadership, will, single-mindedness, and the pride and power of standing apart, of being a law unto themselves. Almost every animal on Earth has its own symbolism defined by mythic tradition, but the interpretation of these symbols is up to the person experiencing them.

Being aware of the synchronicity in your life is a recognition of the interconnectedness of the unseen force, which is probably what we call God. Examples of synchronicity can even be found in the arts. *The China Syndrome* is a fictional movie about a nuclear disaster in which an atomic power plant suffers a meltdown. Just three weeks after the film's debut, the incident became reality at Pennsylvania's infamous Three Mile Island nuclear facility.

Synchronicities of staggering magnitude give us proof that there is something invisible at work. We begin to rethink the nature of time itself. We can viscerally feel that there is no past or present or future. Instead, all time is happening concurrently and eternally. As Einstein said, "Men invented time to feel comfortable in space. But it doesn't actually exist. *All* experience is happening at once." Perhaps our entire soul's experience over lifetimes might be inextricably locked into the universal organizing God principle's existence. We are all, therefore, woven together in the same God fabric. All we have to do is recognize it. Synchronicities, then, are the connections between that spiritual world always turning behind the scenes of this physical one, like the backstage goings-on of a play that the audience is not really aware of.

And then we have reincarnation, a favorite subject of mine. Although very much believed in the East, in the West it is beginning to be more and more regarded as a potential possibility. A friend of mine, Stephen Hawking, the man who saw black holes as a result of his internal journey within himself because he suffers from ALS, a motor neuron disease, went on national television to say that reincarnation was a distinct possibility because of coincidences that had haunted him since childhood. While just a grammar school student, he learned that Galileo, the great Italian mathematician, astronomer, and physicist, died January 8, 1642, three hundred years to the day before Hawking was born. He was suggesting that the soul of Galileo got reincarnated in himself, the modern English scientist. I, of course, and many other people have had many synchronistic events relating to believing that we have been born and died and lived before, but that's a whole other discussion.

People who continually experience meaningful coincidences and acknowledge them believe that synchronicity in all its forms is a kind of personal guidance—a kind of God-like direction that takes us into the future, and if we choose to follow the guidance, our personal destinies evolve and become clear. Joseph Campbell defined it as "following our truth" regardless of consequences, making for ourselves the authentic life, then living the hero's journey according to our own values, which share little or nothing with popular values. If we follow our bliss, as Joseph Campbell said, our *moira,* a term the Greeks used to define higher destiny, we will be doing what we feel most inwardly qualified and inclined to do, regardless of the social and material consequences.

Meaningful coincidences are truly extraordinary, and when we are aware of them, they can exert major shifts in our individual psychological condition. There are profoundly revealing flashes of self-recognition which, once we behold them, make an indelible impression on our personality. Carl Jung, when treating his patients, said the degree of their psychosis stood in direct relation to their level of spiritual convictions. If they lacked religious beliefs, philosophic or spiritual views, they had the deepest neurosis. By restoring his patients' lost spirituality, he improved their condition. He concluded that a spiritual instinct is part of the human psyche.

Modern science reduces existence to a depersonalized mechanism. But the gap between science and spirituality is being bridged by the recognition that our visible physical reality is connected to an invisible spiritual reality. That is quantum mechanics, quantum physics. Some quantum physicists are attempting to prove that spirit and consciousness exist equally in a physically materialistic world. The quantum physicists are the new priests of today. If they say it's real—then it's real.

If we valued more our burgeoning spiritual instincts, perhaps many of our problems would fall away. Perhaps many of us wouldn't feel so alienated from society and ourselves. Recognizing and trusting this spiritual instinct could help us relate with more balance to a clearly neurotic society. Just being aware of a synchronistic event in one's life is an immediate infusion of spiritual instinct, brought about through individual recognition of the unseen spiritual world. There is a connection there that gives us comfort. Nothing is more heart-convincing than personal experience, because it goes deeper than our rational mind can process. It touches the soul. Some individuals doubt that they even own a soul because they have never recognized its existence. Acknowledging synchronicity has the power to shake a person into awareness of the soul. It is the key to unlocking the reality of spiritual existence. In connecting with the synchronicity in our lives, we are again capable of what the Greeks called "catharsis," a purging of the human soul when encountering the divine. At such moments we are convinced of the verity of our own souls because we feel them, experience them. To paraphrase Joseph Campbell: The soul of the human is where the inner and outer worlds meet. Also, awareness of synchronicity instills compassion for all living things because it helps us to see that each one is an important piece in the growing mosaic of Creation, which is an unfinished artwork that would be diminished by the loss of a single fragment. Synchronicity may be thought of as its own religion, the every-man religion, if only because synchronistic events happen to every human being and the cathedral of God lies within the human heart.

Synchronicity is religion without dogma, wherein all are free to draw their own conclusions from personal experience. Appreciation of the synchronicity in our lives gives us spiritual self-confidence and engenders philosophical investigation. Our physical world stands in relation to the unseen spiritual dimension in the same way that a musical sound track underscores the action and drama in a feature film. Absorbed in the story on the screen, the audience is really unaware of the score except when the music swells to make a point. Subconsciously, of course, everyone closely following the motion picture constantly keys into corresponding universally understood musical symbols that imprint the film's predetermined mood on the emotions of its spectators. So, too, the spiritual matrix of our own life story goes largely unseen, but it is felt subconsciously except in dramatic moments of synchronicity. In other words, spiritual power is the sound track of our existence, where every fortissimo is a meaningful synchronicity.

Ralph Waldo Emerson wrote that the greatest discoveries are those we make about ourselves. There is no more effective means of making those self-discoveries than embracing the synchronicity that punctuates our earthly existence. Its value derives from the assumption that everything you need or want to know lies within yourself, and the assessing of synchronicity will bring you the kind of discoveries Emerson esteemed as most precious. They are empowering experiences that inspire us to take up the hero's journey in search of our destiny. By keeping a journal, by applying the simple techniques of interpretation and integration, by recording our dreams, by jotting down every synchronistic event that may happen in our lives, we will be on our own Grail quest toward the authentic life with the God Source as our cocreative inner partner. The more we pay attention to synchronicity in our lives, and the more we record it so we can look at it later, the more we see that our lives will improve and our destiny will unfold as it was meant to be.

# chapter

4

WHEN I MOVED INTO MY NEW HOUSE, I WAS CONCERNED NOT
only about the physical wellness of the house (roof, drains, etc.),
but also the physical wellness of my own body. I have a ranch in
Abiquiu, New Mexico, where Georgia O'Keeffe used to paint. I
have lived there for fifteen years and never had trouble with juni-
per pollen. When I bought this new house in Santa Fe, I had no
idea that allergies would soon prevent me from even visiting my
ranch. The synchronicity of buying a house in Santa Fe saved me
from taking up permanent residence in New Mexican clinics due
to allergies and my inability to breathe in Abiquiu. The synchronicity of ageing has resulted in my putting my creative show business and film life on the blurry back burner of memory so I can
focus on what is wrong with me now.

Because of my allergies I have had to educate myself about
my overall physical condition, which has led me to investigate
allopathic medicine (that is, traditional Western), as opposed to
alternative medicine in this country.

I have been blessed in my life to be healthy. Good genes, exercise from dancing, and a fairly balanced diet. So to experience anything physically wrong has been difficult for me.

My surgeries have been expected. Knee surgery from dancing, neck surgery (from sticking it out, I would say), kidney surgery for a cyst that wasn't cancerous, and a face-lift when I was fifty. All in all, that's not too much anesthetic. But lately I've been having such problems with allergies that I thought it was causing very bad acid reflux.

*Death by Modern Medicine* is not just the name of a book by Carolyn Dean (whom I will quote extensively). It's a condition afflicting doctors and patients. The statistics are staggering. From 1990 to 2000 about 7 to 8 million people suffered death by medicine. There have been thousands of fatalities linked to the drug Vioxx (prescribed to me after my neck surgery). Close to one third of the millions of women who took fen-phen to lose weight suffered heart or lung damage. Celebrex causes heart disease as do other nonsteroidal anti-inflammatory drugs. Suicides are occurring resulting from Prozac, and the list goes on.

All of these treatments focus on treating the symptoms, not the cause. Drug companies thrive when people remain sick. Modern medicine itself is the number one cause of death every year. The figure is 784,000 deaths a year due to medicine-related causes. That's 2,150 deaths a day just in this country alone.

Medical doctors are licensed and regulated by their own medical boards, and increasingly these boards are populated with representatives of the drug industry and doctors who are paid advisers for the drug companies.

The failure of modern medicine began with its overriding

desire to create a monopoly. Documentation goes back to the time of Henry VIII, when allopathic (another word for "conventional") doctors convinced the city of London to pass a bylaw requiring a license to practice as a way of controlling herbalists. Women who were herbalists, midwives, and healers were burned at the stake for allegedly practicing witchcraft.

In North America, doctors are in the upper echelons of society, sit on government benches, and create laws and regulations to benefit themselves. In early modern-day medicine, homeopathy, osteopathy, and chiropractic, naturopathic treatments, etc., were frowned upon, but today there is so much suspicion of allopathic medicine that patients resort to spending $21 billion a year for alternative medicine.

In conventional care, we have five-minute medicine. We wait two months for an appointment, one hour in the waiting room, twenty minutes in the examining room, for five minutes with the doctor. Rarely do we find family doctors anymore who know us and our families. Now everyone is a specialist. Medicine has become a servant of the technology of drugs instead of a healing art.

The separation between mind, body, and spirit has never been more obvious than in modern medicine. There is no education in medical training that the three are connected. In fact, most doctors will laugh at such a notion. Nutrition and emotional stress are not really considered relevant to a person's physical maladies.

Every nutritionist I've ever met in a hospital is overweight and underaware of it. When my mother was recovering from surgery, the nutritionist came in with her lunch tray, which consisted of a Coke, a cheeseburger, chocolate cake, and ice cream. When

I looked up at her in astonishment, she said, "It's good for the patient because it makes her think she'll feel better." The woman weighed about two hundred pounds. In horror, I watched her waddle away.

For many people vitamins and supplements are extremely beneficial, but the medical and drug industries are attempting to move them into a drug category so that prescriptions are necessary. Monopoly of medicine and censorship are a way slowly but surely to erode the beneficial effect on human health outside of the accepted allopathic drug industry.

Why does modern medicine treat alternative cures with such shabby cynicism? The preferred treatments in Europe and Asia are supplements: herbal, homeopathic, and holistic. A holistic doctor treats the mind, body, and spirit. He knows they are connected and one affects the other.

Our advertising and media contribute to how we heal ourselves. We are inundated with electronic information waves of every description. The advertising world is a scientific operation, and we are being advertised to death. We smoke, drink, overeat, and stress out as we rush to a yoga class and give ourselves only twenty minutes to meditate. We use our computers, cell phones, and Palm Pilots, ingesting all of those electromagnetic waves as we pop diet pills to look as though we are healthy.

It's no secret that we all fear disease. But we should remember that disease is dis-ease. The word itself is a clue to what's going on. We are being propagandized from every corner of our free society.

Alex Carey, a psychologist, said it best: "The twentieth century has been characterized by three developments of great political importance: the growth of democracy, the growth of corporate power, and the growth of corporate propaganda as a means of protecting corporate power against democracy."

The most manipulative propaganda is that modern medicine has anything to do with health. Drug companies who make sick pills for healthy people also make a lot of money.

When I had profound pain three months after my neck surgery, my surgeon (one of the best regarding surgery, one of the worst regarding sensitivity) wouldn't even answer the phone. He left a message with his assistant: "Tell her to take Vioxx." It turned out that I had a compacted rib bone from stress.

I have come to understand that I should approach the food that I eat as I would a medicine or drug. It's that important. Yet our food is being polluted by pesticides, herbicides, and fungicides. I eat only organic fruits and vegetables but that doesn't mean they are not hybrid. I try to live without the whites: bread, sugar, flour, and pasta. I eat chicken and fish, hopefully raised without antibiotics. But how can we really tell?

My big problem in my life is my sweet tooth. I've had it since childhood. At times I am insulin resistant, which basically means I have an inability to transport sugar into the cells. The result is high blood levels of sugar and insulin. Chronically elevated insulin helps create obesity and, worse than anything, keeps me from losing weight. I do my workout every day and basically don't eat much, but to lose weight? It's a nightmare!

Death by sugar is clear, but a war on sugar . . . I don't have the trained troops.

Dr. Nancy Appleton is a researcher and nutritional consultant who has made a life study of sugar and why we should wage war on it. She has compiled a mind-blowing list of 136 ways sugar is harmful to your health to prove her point.

Here is a list of conditions that are triggered or worsened by high sugar intake:

1. Cardiac arrhythmia PMS (progesterone levels disturbed)

2. Fatigue

3. Insomnia

4. Panic attacks

5. Hypertension

6. The "alphabet soup" of autoimmune diseases, e.g., MS, MG

There are ten teaspoons of sugar in a can of soda pop and twenty-seven teaspoons in a milk shake.

Sugar-free substitutes are just as bad in different ways. Aspartame (NutraSweet) is a neurotoxin and should be avoided completely. Studies link it to birth defects, brain tumors, and seizures and say that it contributes to diabetes and emotional disorders. We should avoid any synthetic sweeteners and use honey instead. That means no Splenda, Equal, saccharin, or Sweet 'N Low. Stevia is okay if it's natural.

Sugar is a legalized poison, and I try my best to be poison-free. I use honey on my cereal and have one bite of dessert from someone else's plate when I'm out to dinner. I don't eat the fat on chicken or fish, and rarely eat red meat anyway. My carbs come from vegetables and fruit. I've given up pasta and bread and am not happy about it at all. For salt I use Kymalazan or Celtic Sea Salt, which is not processed and is delicious.

I've allowed my yoga practice to be a glory of the past because I do so much other exercise (weight lifting, stretching, mountain hiking, and stomach exercising). But I still believe yoga is a miraculous discipline. Yoga itself means "union," a union of balance, strength, and flexibility. Another discipline I do is Xi Gong. I do spontaneous Xi Gong, which means I stand very relaxed on the floor, allow my intelligent mind to take a backseat, and I get out of a disciplinarian mind frame and allow my body to move in whatever way it chooses to. I'm fascinated by the ways my body wants to move. Sometimes it is gentle, as I find myself swaying slowly as I watch my arms rotate in ways that tell me they have an intelligence of their own. It always makes me aware that the body is basically energy, and the energy tells me it needs to move in certain configurations to stay balanced. Sometimes my arms and legs and torso move for long periods of time and sometimes not. I notice that if something is physically bothering me (aches and pains from exercise or cold or even a restless night), the movement itself acts as a healer because it redistributes the energy, which contributes to the balance of my whole system.

I think the reason I've never really been sick in my life is because I've led a drug-free existence. I always have. I've never done a line of coke or taken any drugs for recreation. But once Robert Mitchum gave me some bang brownies, and I thought I was walking around in my own brain cells (fascinating, by the way). And I smoked pot in a hotel room in London, and afterward nearly ate the furniture, I was so hungry. At a fancy dinner party in Hollywood, I put a teaspoon of what I thought was very refined sugar in my demitasse coffee. The hostess was horrified, because it was a thousand dollars' worth of coke. I didn't drink the coffee, and I was never invited back.

I naively wondered why so many of my show business friends would congregate in bathrooms with the windows open and come out looking like they'd dunked their faces in powdered sugar doughnuts. So I have no education in the drug world. I am a novice. And where prescription drugs are concerned, I've taken antibiotics a few times, and every now and then 2 mg of Valium to sleep. I do take melatonin. It's calming before bed and wonderful for the hair.

Alternative medicine has become a bridge to other realities we know very little about in the West. It comes, I think, from a basic distrust in the limited thinking of conventional doctors. Millions of people are taking active steps to venture outside the medical mainstream with acupuncture, herbal treatments, homeopathy, supplements, and holistic points of view in general. Forty-eight percent of American adults, according to the *New York Times,* use at least one alternative or complementary therapy. The percentage continues to grow every year. They feel their overall well-being is not being addressed. They are looking for ways to assist the body in its own capacity to fight off disease and heal. More and more people are learning to use their own intuition as to their bodies and mind, body, spirit connections. People who follow naturopathic techniques find fewer drug side effects, unhurried service, more affectionate care, and say they feel they are being treated as whole persons, not persons with specific symptoms.

I have had a hiatal hernia, which caused me severe acid reflux for many years. It was recommended that I take Prilosec to decrease the hydrochloric acid. I took the Prilosec for years until I began seriously to question the role of hydrochloric acid in our bodies. If we have such an abundance of this acid, isn't there likely some reason for it to be there in the first place? Do we need a natural amount of hydrochloric acid for proper digestion?

Some doctors say that an infant who is not breast-fed in the first twelve hours will suffer digestive tract maladies later in life because the digestive computer isn't turned on by the colostrum in mother's milk. I wasn't breast-fed, which I came to realize might have been the reason for my digestive computer problems. (There is a reason why nature meant for mothers to breast-feed their children immediately.)

I began to make a study of what the digestive tract meant to my human health. My research led me to understand that the seat of my health resides with the "inner terrain" of my body, which is governed by digestion.

Our bodies are alkaline by design and acid by function. Maintaining a proper balance is essential for life, health, and vitality. Without the alkaline balance, our "inner terrain" is a breeding ground for bacteria, yeast, and other unwanted organisms. I found that all leading biochemists and medical physiologists recognize that our pH balance (acid-alkaline balance) is the most important aspect of a balanced and healthy body. Our digestive tracts have varying degrees of acid by design and our urinary tracts should be slightly acidic for healthy function.

My pH had been out of whack for many years, and I was taking a proton pump inhibitor (a drug like Prilosec or Nexium, acid depressors) which was alleviating the burning acid, but at what cost? My doctors saw nothing wrong with 40 mg in the morning and 40 mg at night, until it began to become evident in patients over fifty that there was a correlation between heartburn drugs and more and more broken hips and fractures. Broken bones and fractures in the elderly often lead to life-threatening complications.

Patients over fifty who used acid-reducing drugs for more than a year had a 44 percent higher risk of hip fractures than nonusers. The longer the patient took the drugs, the higher their risk.

Most people do not take enough calcium to start with. Add the lack of calcium absorption, and there is a real problem. Women over sixty taking heartburn drugs put themselves at risk of developing osteoporosis.

I soon understood I needed to get off the drug. (Nexium, which is similar to Prilosec, is the second-most-profitable drug in the world with global sales of $4.6 billion a year, as reported by IMS Health, which tracks drug sales.)

So I was learning that I—and everyone else who had digestive problems—was at war within myself. We were becoming more and more susceptible to bacteria, fungus, yeasts, and molds.

I found I had developed a bad cough and was more bothered by allergies than ever before. I needed to take my pH imbalance seriously and get off the heartburn drugs.

The germs were nothing; my inner terrain was everything.

Because of the animosity that the AMA and the pharmaceutical companies have in general for alternative healing procedures, I am going to be deliberately careful with the specifics of how I've healed myself. I am disguising the doctors' names because they could lose their licenses if their work is seen as too expert and successful!

I reconnected with a naturopathic dentist whom I had known for twenty-five years. He had become a researcher in what is called "energy medicine" and had been practicing with much success as a doctor. His knowledge of teeth was instrumental in furthering his research because he understood that each tooth in the human mouth is connected to a meridian energy line that connects to various organs in the body. But I don't want to get ahead of my story.

Dr. Lin took my case, which was: I had allergies, horrible acid reflux, and some problems dealing with menopause.

Dr. Lin is a spiritual dowser. That means he uses a dowsing rod, which is literally and physically moved by his own spiritual guides to diagnose the maladies in a patient. It was fascinating to watch how it worked.

I was used to dowsing techniques because I had employed dowsers to locate underground water on my ranch in New Mexico. The water dowser simply holds his rod over the ground as he walks the property. Whenever it moves and points down, we know water is there. When he asks how many feet below the surface, the rod will respond by moving up and down. My water dowser was never wrong. He said he didn't know if it was his own higher knowledge of the location of water or whether it was a spiritual guide of his. He learned it all from an Indian shaman.

So as I watched the dowsing techniques of Dr. Lin, I quickly realized I had to know enough medically to ask the right questions. So did Dr. Lin.

I began by wanting to know what the operating level of hydrochloric acid was in my body. The dowsing rod moved eighteen times, which according to Dr. Lin meant that I had only 18 percent efficacy of what my hydrochloric acid should be. The Prilosec had reduced the effectiveness of my acid down to 18 percent. No wonder I didn't have heartburn anymore! But at what cost? I was coughing all the time. I felt weak. I wasn't sleeping, and my allergies were terrible.

I agreed with Dr. Lin I should get off the Prilosec right away or a hip fracture could be next, according to the statistics.

I was nervous at first because I knew the heartburn would return, as the body would endeavor to restore its acid, which was needed for the functioning of so many other things.

I went cold turkey off the Prilosec. Dr. Lin gave me a formula that tasted like chalk in powder form. Whenever I mixed a half a teaspoon of it in water and swallowed, the heartburn went away. I'm not sure what was in the chalklike powder. I was told it was a process of $H_2O$, which meant another version of water to me, so I really don't know what to say except that it worked.

I took a half teaspoon of the "chalk" in water whenever I was bothered by heartburn, and I must say I was fine.

My hydrochloric acid began to return, and the last time I checked it was close to what it should be in order to restore a balanced alkaline and acid "inner terrain" in my body.

I'm careful with how much protein from fish, meat, and fowl I eat because it galvanizes the hydrochloric acid back into action. For me, a third-world diet is the best: one-third protein, one-third carbs, and one-third fruits and vegetables.

After my healing was in full swing, I learned how to make my own homeopathic remedies with a portable machine that Dr. Lin purchased for me. I mix a sample of whatever mold or spores or pollen I remove from the trees around where I live with a little bit of my own urine in a shot glass and place the glass on one side of the machine. On the other side I place a dropper bottle full of sterilized water. I turn on the machine, wait for it to do its work, and within a few minutes the energy of the contents of the shot glass has transferred to the homeopathic water, and I have my remedy. It's quite an amazing medical and natural process and, most of all, it is working.

I take this machine with me wherever I am in the world and

use my urine mixed with whatever pollutants may be in the air in the shot glass and wait for the machine to transfer the energy of the shot glass into the bottle of water, which makes my own homeopathic remedy. It's a procedure known as "radionics" and is without the side effects of allopathic medicine. I have to be careful not to allow the homeopathic remedy to go through security at the airport because the energy of the security machines neutralizes the remedy. That's why I take the machine with me. I know I can rely on it.

If Terry picks up a mold, or something is in her dander, I include some of her dog hairs in the shot glass and anything else I think may be causing my allergies.

If I were to ask now what is making me sick, I would know that acidosis is the answer. A state of acidosis is simply the lack of oxygen and available calcium, which the body uses to maintain its alkaline balance. I know now that an acidic, anaerobic (lacking oxygen) body environment encourages the breeding of fungus, mold, bacteria, and viruses.

On the other hand if I don't have a balance of enough acid (which I didn't because of the Prilosec), I'm in trouble, too. Calcium makes up 1.6 percent of our body weight. It is literally the human glue that holds the body together. Calcium is used by the body to maintain its alkaline balance. Calcium is so biochemically active that it has been likened to an octopus. A calcium ion can hold on to seven other molecules while it grabs on to one molecule of water. No other ion can do this. And it is the right size to get in and out of the human cell easily. As it does this, it takes a chain of nutrients into the cell, then leaves to get more nutrients.

Our lives depend on our biological inner terrain. In other words there are really no specific diseases, there are only specific disease conditions.

The human body is very intelligent, and I am learning to rely more and more on its intelligence rather than drugs.

If I am properly alkaline, I feel stronger, my energy is higher, and my mind functions more effectively. I also have more memory. When I am acidic, my immune system doesn't function as well, my energy is low, and my mind can't focus properly.

This inner terrain balance depends on many things. But probably the most important is diet. In making a study of which foods were more alkaline in the body and which were acidic, I was stunned. For example, all citrus fruits and juices turn alkaline in the system even though they are acid when we drink them. Meat, fish, fowl, and most animal products turn acidic. All vegetables, except cooked tomatoes, turn alkaline.

So we should observe a diet that is 20 percent acidic and 80 percent alkaline. There are several good books written by experts on the subject that can guide us on what to eat, but here are some quick tips for those days when you just can't get your pH up. Some of what I'm going to share with you will surprise you. Some of it may make you laugh. But try it and be amazed at the difference you feel.

1. Just before you step out of the shower, turn the temperature of the water down. It should be tepid to cool. Cool water is alkalizing. (Think about the Scandinavians who jump from a hot tub into a snowbank. They are on to something!)

2. If you have a cold, flu, respiratory illness, or allergies, make a pot of vegetable soup. Add no meat, chicken, or meat or chicken stock. Put in every kind of fresh vegetable you have on hand

and season with a dash of sea salt. Have a cup of your soup every hour until you begin to feel better, and you begin to test alkaline. Microbes and viruses cannot exist in an alkaline body.

3. Make lemonade. As odd as it sounds, lemons, as acidic as they are, actually alkalinize the body. I prefer a cup of warm water with the juice of half a fresh lemon. I usually throw the squeezed lemon right in the cup. Warm or cold, it works.

4. Have a banana instead of a candy bar. Bananas are naturally alkalizing and will not affect the glucose levels of the body as severely as sugar.

5. Snack on dried fruits such as raisins, apricots, and dates.

6. Include almonds, Brazil nuts, and walnuts in your snacks.

7. There are only two grains that are alkalizing: corn meal, which can create glucose level issues for some, and quinoa. Eat or bake with these grains whenever possible. Avoid white flour!

8. Drink water. Good ol' $H_2O$ is very alkalizing.

9. Have a cup of green tea instead of a cup of coffee.

10. Try to get ten minutes of morning sun every day. Research indicates that vitamin D, which most of us don't get an ample supply of anymore, helps the body store alkalizing nutrients.

11. Take a moment, whether you are at work, in the
    office, or at play, to breathe and visualize. Inhale
    through the nose, exhale through the mouth.
    Keep your shoulders back and your back straight.
    Take each breath in slowly and exhale slowly.
    Visualize all the acidic toxins being exhaled from
    your body.

12. Alkalize by the foods you eat! Incorporate more
    of the foods in these lists in your daily regime and
    feel the changes in your body!

    *Vegetables:* Beet greens, beets, broccoli, cabbage,
    carrots, cauliflower, celery, chard greens, chilis, collard
    greens, edible flowers, eggplant, garlic, green beans,
    green peas, kale, kohlrabi, lettuce, mushrooms,
    mustard greens, onions, parsnips, peppers, pumpkin,
    radishes, rutabaga, spinach, sprouts, sweet potatoes,
    tomatoes, watercress

    *Fruits:* Apples, apricots, avocados, bananas, berries,
    cantaloupe, cherries, coconut (fresh), dates, figs,
    grapes, grapefruit, honeydew melon, lemon, lime,
    nectarines, oranges, peaches, pears, pineapple, plums,
    raisins, rhubarb, strawberries, tangerines, tomato,
    watermelon

    *Nuts and Seeds:* Almonds, chestnuts, walnuts, flax
    seeds, pumpkin seeds, sunflower seeds

I know this is quite a bit to "digest" . . . but keeping an alka-
lized body will help you feel your best.

Once my healing of the inner terrain was in progress, I began to learn the importance of our teeth. I was more astonished at what I learned about teeth than anything else.

Our eyes may be the window to our souls, but to know about our physical health we should open our mouths wide and look inside. As someone said to me, "It's all in your head!"

Every time we brush our teeth, especially if there is any inflammation in the mouth, it puts bacteria into our bloodstream. Dental problems, receding or inflamed gums, cavities, tooth loss, gingivitis, and other dental dilemmas in adults can indicate the presence of serious health problems in the rest of the body, including heart disease, diabetes, cancer, vitamin deficiencies, and even the risk of having a premature or low-birthweight baby.

Often it's a naturopathic dentist who is the first to identify a systemic health problem because of what he or she finds in a patient's mouth. After forty years of research, the great German physician Dr. Reinhard Voll estimated that nearly 80 percent of all illness in the human body is connected in some way to problems in the mouth. Oral toxicity has also been shown to be the cause of much anxiety, depression, hyperactivity, and suicidal behavior as well as other psychological conditions.

All teeth are linked to the body through the energy/acupuncture meridians. Root canals, amalgam fillings, nonprecious crowns, or any substance that is not compatible with the body may create an "interference field," blocking or altering the energy flow of the associated meridian. Such a blockage results in a lack of energetic nourishment and physical symptoms in an organ or body function remote from the tooth.

When a tooth is diseased, the dentist has the choice of taking the tooth out or doing a root canal treatment. These days, a dentist will usually offer to treat the abscess, deal with the pain, and save the tooth. This is where opinions split as to what is best to do. Do we look to save individual teeth or do we look to treat the whole patient?

That is what happened to me.

I was having a toothache in my lower wisdom tooth on the left side when I went to Dr. Lin. Being a naturopathic dentist he educated me as to the important connections between each tooth and the body's overall health or sickness. My wisdom tooth was directly connected to the acupuncture meridian to my stomach and all my attendant problems with digestion.

Long story short, I had the tooth removed by a cavitation process by another dentist. Cavitation removal is not taught in schools of dentistry. The common belief is that just pulling the tooth that aches removes the problem. I learned differently.

Under the aching tooth, deep down in the bone, there was a bad infection, which was blocking the energy flow of the stomach meridian. Cavitation removal is not just the process of removing the tooth but also scraping out the bacteria and infection that reside in the bone underneath. In my case much of the bone needed to be removed. After that, my digestive problems cleared up.

I won't go into specifics here about which tooth goes into which meridian to organs in the body, but at the end of this book you will find a very useful chart detailing this. If you are interested in a further exploration, I encourage you to look into naturopathic dentistry.

I was interested in how osteoporosis was connected to tooth disease and found that osteoporosis and tooth loss often go hand in hand because the same decrease in bone mineral density that boosts the risk of hip and other fractures affects the jawbone and teeth. That's one reason older women are especially vulnerable to tooth loss following menopause and why hormone replacement therapy became so popular even though the doctors still don't seem to know what to do about their recommendations. I say, fix the teeth!

There are apparently four stages in a female's life when she is most vulnerable to oral problems: puberty, monthly periods, pregnancy, and menopause. Certain hormone levels are elevated, which stimulates inflammatory mediators that make them more susceptible and responsive to bacteria in the mouth. So we should mark our calendars and have dental exams during any of these times. But the exams should be done by dentists who understand the connections between the teeth and the acupuncture meridians to the organs. Toothaches and other oral problems are caused by the stagnation of circulation within the meridians that travel to the oral cavities. The meridians that lead from the stomach and intestines are usually the ones treated when we have toothaches. Acupuncture therapy can alleviate some of the problems and pain, but cavitation is recommended to cut the disease away. The disease is not only in the tooth, it is also in the bone. And much of the reason for that is that the inner terrain of the body itself does not have an equal alkaline and acid balance.

I learned the hard way. My tooth (and much of the bone beneath it) is gone and my digestion is much better. I had all but two of my silver fillings removed some years ago. But as we now know, silver fillings are really mercury, and most everyone knows what mercury does to the system and its inner terrain. The wisdom tooth I had removed was one of the remaining mercury fillings.

The reason the teeth are such a threat to our health is that, in addition to their connections to every organ and gland in the body, they can harbor infections without symptoms—there is no pain or discomfort very often, yet there may be chronic infection eroding the body's immune response, wearing out the immune system. And this infection is very difficult to detect. I had had the infection long before the toothache. About 98 percent of Americans have some areas of diseased gum tissue in their mouths, and half of these are also experiencing a progressive "bone loss."

The mouth, unfortunately for those who like to kiss, is a hostile environment. It's warm, moist, and full of nutrient-laden saliva, decaying teeth, and saggy gums, which makes a haven for bacteria.

The philosophy underlying the teaching of dentistry today, in the main, limits its practice to mechanics, pain control, and aesthetics. I was fortunate in finding naturopathic doctors and dentists who could *really* help me. I was fortunate to meet and be helped by Dr. Bill Wolfe. He practices in Santa Fe, and I urge you, dear Reader, if you are having tooth problems, to go to his website at www.drwolfe.com.

Along with my wisdom tooth problem I have three root canal teeth that are on the meridian points to my stomach and lungs. I thought perhaps I should have the root canal teeth pulled, but Dr. Wolfe tested the toxicity of the teeth and found that they weren't bad enough for removal. He suggested laser treatment for me so that I could save the teeth. I seem to be doing fine now, but without the laser treatment I think my immune system would have suffered.

As Dr. Voll says, we have only so much currency in our immune system bank accounts. If our immune systems are always concentrating on keeping our teeth healthy, some other part of the body is paying the price with neglect.

I am grateful I have come to understand the naturopathic

way of looking at my health. Unfortunately, the vast majority of states in the U.S. do not recognize naturopathic care of any kind, so it is difficult to get your insurance to cover your treatment. It is a shame that most insurance companies do not recognize the long-range benefits of such care.

As we all know, vitamins, herbs, and supplements are not regulated by the FDA, and therefore are not covered by insurance companies. Lab tests for patients using alternative care are not covered in most instances unless administered by an allopathic physician.

The Naturopathic Doctors Association recommends contacting your insurance company and asking (1) what they cover in the alternative medicine field, (2) why they don't cover more, and (3) for them to please cover all forms of naturopathic and alternative care for medical and dental.

I can afford alternative care without my insurance covering it. But for those who can't—it's a crime on every level. It's time we reeducate our human health system to include alternative and complementary systems of treatment. The Cleveland Clinic in Cleveland, Ohio, is proposing just that. They are in the initial stages of building a clinic for complementary and alternative medicine, and they've asked me to be a part of it, which I'm very excited about.

I'm reminded of Dr. Benjamin Rush, a signer of the Declaration of Independence. He wrote: "Unless we put Medical Freedom into the Constitution, the time will come when medicine will organize into an undercover dictatorship . . . to restrict the art of healing to one class of men, and deny equal privilege to others, will be to constitute the Bastille of Medical Science. All such laws are un-American and despotic and have no place in a Republic . . . The Constitution of this Republic should make special privilege for Medical Freedom as well as Religious Freedom."

# chapter
# 5

I'M SITTING IN MY NEW LIBRARY. I'VE UNPACKED MOST OF MY books and Terry is sitting on one. The library has high ceilings and floor-to-ceiling bookshelves completely covering two of the walls. The books seem to look down on me as they are reflected in the soft light of the fireplace.

Some of the books on the high shelves were left to me by Vera Zorina. They are books about subjects I never delved into because I didn't go to college. I was too busy being successful in show business. I think Vera Zorina wanted me to live in this house because she wanted to leave her books to me. Between the two of us, I now have books relating to nearly every subject on Earth (and beyond) and finally have a room where they can all live together on their shelves, available to teach me when I contemplate all my questions. I have a great respect for the written word. A long time ago I learned as an actress that "if it's not on the page, it's not on the stage!"

I have many books on the time period of Atlantis. Please bear with me, dear Reader, and keep an open mind as I tell you

I believe that I lived on the lost continent of Atlantis. My belief is based on vivid past-life memories that I was able to access during past-life therapy. These memories come in the form of pictures, which inspire deep emotional reactions. I am not hypnotized, which many people find easier and beneficial. No, I lie on a couch, a comfortable place to relax, and allow my higher self to show me more of what I have inherited in my soul's memory. The process is extremely revealing. I have tried for years to put together a film depicting my life and experience when I lived in Atlantis. I did my research from Solon's and Plato's writings in Greece, the teachings of Edgar Cayce, the works of Frank Joseph and Chirawood, my studies of archeology in Egypt, and the memories I have had of the past from my own meditations and past-life therapy. There are nights when the memories are so vivid with intense color that I wake up. I don't know if I am dreaming the past or remembering it. And what does it matter? In my maturing years I realize how important it is to acknowledge our pasts lest we make the same mistakes. And Atlantis was part of my past in my reality.

I believe we all have soul memory. I love the fact that the older I get, the more soul memory I have. I see now what is meant by long-term memory as opposed to short-term memory. I have no short-term memory anymore for nearly anything. It's extremely disconcerting. I think sometimes I wouldn't be able to pass a test for a new driver's license. Sometimes I remember more about who I *was* than who I *am*!

But I'm learning to relax into the flow of what might not be so important anymore. So what if I can't remember a name or my own address. This defect comes in handy being an actor: I *have* to inhabit a character completely now, or I'll never remember the lines!

I approach it all as an imaginative septuagenarian and have to conclude that on some level, even imagination is real, if only because it's symbolic. I had a father then in Atlantis who was my father this time around. I had a daughter who is my daughter now, and I had a lover and husband, both of whom I have known now except their identities were reversed. I remember the drama of our relationships then, which also impact our relationships today. Everyone has her dramas today and, I believe, has had similar dramas in the past with the same souls. However, to resolve the emotional issues, a soul who may have been an enemy in the past could be a friend today. The intent is to clear out the karma (what one puts out, one gets back).

The art of theater and film bears out such a truth. A script doesn't work unless karma is served. The bad people must pay or the film or play doesn't work. During my past life in Atlantis, I remember the high-tech sophisticated technologies revolving mostly around the hidden power of crystal energy. I remember cultural exchanges with extraterrestrials who preferred, then as now, to be called star visitors. The drama of my life then centered around a daughter who was essentially on her own, her father who abandoned us both, and a lover of mine who was deeply involved with the star visitors. Ultimately, he boarded a craft and left. I remember being crestfallen because I wanted to go, too. Yes, this may seem like crazy imagination, of course, but what if it's true? What if all imagination is true on some level? I have my imagination because I'm a searcher for truth regardless of how bizarre it may sound to others whose imaginations and truths are only different, not right or wrong.

I feel that, having been a survivor, I now want to become an evolver.

So I did a great deal of research on Atlantis. According to Edgar Cayce (the famous American seer), there was a huge continent somewhere in the Atlantic Ocean that underwent a series of inundations . . . huge catastrophes over time . . . the last inundation being about thirty-two hundred years ago. According to Cayce and others, Atlantis existed for more than one hundred thousand years, during which there were many upheavals. It had to rebuild itself many times, just as we have had to do in modern times. In our Western civilization, we went through the Dark Ages and before that the classical civilization which was all but forgotten with the fall of the Roman Empire. Then we rebuilt it to achieve the Renaissance. According to Cayce and others, Atlantis was a highly developed culture that existed far deeper in the past than any of us can even imagine. Its downfall was due to a rise in both militarism and materialism. Prior to that it was a culture of spiritual greatness dedicated to achieving a high technology to support and sustain the human spirit. Greed and materialism led to militarism, which led to the need to conquer others rather than living equally bound to spirit.

We seem to have reached that same apex today in the world as we know it, which is basically why I am so interested in whether we are now mirroring the same conflicts that existed in Atlantis. It is common knowledge in metaphysical circles that the United States is known as the New Atlantis, at least according to Sir Francis Bacon (the father of science). He wrote a book entitled *New Atlantis*. A materialistic and militaristic people will always have a failure of culture. Unfortunately, we learn from history that human beings *do not* learn from history.

Cayce claimed that a rising number of souls who had lived in Atlantis would reincarnate in America in the twentieth century. Therefore, the consciousness of people today is rising out of the memory of their souls. As American Atlanteans, we missed the lesson then that we must learn now. Again, we are a global civilization as we were then. What we perpetrate on another today, we in turn perpetrate on ourselves tomorrow.

When I visited Egypt for an extended period of time, I was fascinated to learn from archeologists and researchers how some believed that the pyramids of Egypt and the Sphinx dated back many thousands of years before ancient Egypt came into existence. They achieved their pharaonic greatness, they said, because the "people of the first time" had escaped from a dying Atlantis and helped transfer their knowledge to Egypt. The Atlanteans opined that their culture was dying, and they wanted the divine aspects of it to be preserved. Egyptian archeologists told me (as did my books) that the great Greek lawmaker and thinker Solon had traveled to Egypt, where he was a tourist visiting the temple of Skieo, and there he was educated by the high priest regarding the story of Atlantis, which had been preserved in the ancient Egyptian tablets. That story was taken by Solon back to Greece, where it was passed down eventually to Plato, who wrote about it in *Timaeus* and *Critias*. There was controversy among the experts as to whether Plato was using the Atlantis story as an allegory for materialism and materialistic corruption and decay or whether he believed he was reporting facts. We could say the same thing now. In any case, our American culture is mirroring the Atlantean crumbling from materialism and militaristic decay and corruption.

While in Egypt I went to Medinet Habu or the Victory Temple. It's very well preserved, and hieroglyphics there tell of a leader who had a battle with the "Atlantean Sun Peoples" and how they were captured by him. Running through the stories of Atlantis are references to the star constellation of the Pleiades. The Atlanteans sailed by the position of the Seven Sisters of the Pleiades. "The sweet influences of the Pleiades" is mentioned in the Bible as are "the bands of Orion." The Pleiades were regarded as Atlantis's Daughters of Atlas. They were supposed to be the women who were daughters of a union between Atlas (king of Atlantis) and a sea goddess called Pleione. They had seven daughters, who were so virtuous that they became the seven stars in the Pleiades constellation.

In Atlantis, it was believed then that if man lived according to the laws of Spirit and rhythms of nature he would live happily. If he lived separately from Spirit and nature, he'd create an imbalance. They also believed there is a definite correspondence between human behavior on the Earth and what happens throughout the universe. There is some evidence that the Atlanteans, through their loss of Spiritual laws and addiction to highly advanced technology, tried to use celestial events against their enemies. For example, they tried to use oncoming comets to destroy and wipe out their enemies in nuclear-like events. It is said that because of such abuse, the Atlantean Empire collapsed.

If the Great Flood was part of the Atlantean collapse and sinking, there is ample evidence that it happened. Flood traditions perpetuate throughout the planet and they are basically the same. Joseph Campbell never used the "A" word (Atlantis) because he was known as a prominent scholar and would have gotten a lot of flak. But he did say he felt the great flood stories were something more than the collective unconscious. The enshrining of a myth with such horrendous implications must have happened, he felt.

But he couldn't find scientific proof, so it was too controversial for him to get into. He did, however, bring up the stories in the Mahabarata quite often, which seemed to indicate some kind of battle in the sky.

When you study the flood traditions carefully, the majority of them say there was some kind of disturbance in the heavens, usually associated with the passing of a comet and terrible, flaming debris coming out of the sky. "Fire from heaven" is associated with all flood traditions. But was the fire from comets or man himself? Every Native American myth says their ancestors were not native to the land. They came from another place (survivors of Atlantis?) after the great flood. The Shang Dynasty reported the great flood occurring accompanied by great ash falling from the sky.

For me, these same misuses and abuses apply now. We are warring with competitive technologies, and nature is becoming more and more unbalanced. It is said that the greatest power in the universe is not nuclear or electric or mechanical. By far the greatest power in the entire universe is spiritual power, because it underpins absolutely everything. If we can master our spiritual power, we can do anything, and if we don't learn from our spiritual power, nature will react. Nature wants to be cleansed and balanced. We'll go through the same debacle again if we don't learn from the past.

If we are wiped out by nature again in a global catastrophic event, *we* will be a future myth no less unbelievable than Atlantis is to many today.

The word "Nostrophilia" means a genetic memory usually associated with a place that no longer exists. Birds and animals have been tested to have it. It's ingrained instinctively in their genetic coding. They will return en masse to a place that no longer exists due to a flood or earthquake. They swim or fly to areas in the middle of the ocean, only to perish because they return to something that no longer exists. Japanese scientists have monitored sea and land life that swim or fly to areas in the Atlantic Ocean and die in great numbers because whatever they are returning to no longer exists.

People seem to have "amphysteria" where Atlantis is concerned. "Amphysteria" denotes a condition of forgotten fear, usually about a place. You've forgotten what it is, but you're still afraid of it. I would say the memory of the Atlantean catastrophe is in our genetic coding. People who take very strong positions against the existence of Atlantis, in my opinion, are suffering from amphysteria. It's as though they are afraid to remember an ancient event. Atlantis sank under violent conditions apparently brought about by the people. In my research I found that the ancient Atlanteans were described as red-haired, slightly slanted blue-eyed, and very white-skinned. That caught my attention because of my own appearance. The South American traditions speak of the "Contikivera" culture coming to them after the great flood. They are described as blue-eyed, red-haired, fair, and tall. Several representations of the Ramses III Victory Temple depict the Atlanteans that he captured as tall, with red hair, blue eyes, and white skin.

Perhaps I am hearing the ancient genetic codes of my own soul's journey through time. I take patriotic pride as a Virginian that the Founding Fathers used the Great Pyramid in Egypt as a symbol of unfinished consciousness on the Great Seal of America. Did they, as Masons, believe it could have come from Atlantis?

Part of my Atlantean experience was what I call sexual division. I understand "out of the rib of Adam, Eve was born." However, I don't accept it as a biblical myth. I feel it is true. I hauntingly remember a time when we humans reflected the perfect balance of the soul, a balance of yin and yang. We had achieved a unified state of bliss. Sometimes in meditation I can nearly achieve that state of bliss again today. It's a kind of still point of being where there is no longer anything to learn, no polarity of emotions, an equilibrium that is difficult to hang on to in the harsh reality of life.

Maybe such a state was the original state of being for humans; I don't know. But I remember feeling perfectly peaceful and contented with the fact that I was both male and female, an equal balance of yin and yang. I had both male and female genitalia, but they were not as pronounced as the sexual organs of humans today. I remember reproducing a child through the intention of meditating on the desire to give birth. There was no pain. There was also no elevated sense of joy or negative depression. Those emotions seemed to be false and the polarity of the two a devolution of being. I was peaceful and content, not happy and joyful . . . a state I find myself preferring to be in as I grow older each year. I was a perfectly balanced, harmonious, peaceful, androgynous being.

According to Atlantean experts, the Atlanteans were advanced at genetic engineering. They worshipped the androgyne because it symbolized the unity of opposites, but they became fascinated with observing what would happen if the unity was divided. I remember going through a unity division ceremony conducted by high-priest practitioners using meditation, visualization, and intense color projections. I had agreed to the procedure, which I experienced in a magnificent vat of crystal water. It wasn't like real water. It was thicker and acted as a conductor for the projections of the priest practitioners.

The projected separation began at my head, where I felt my cranium gently separate from itself, yet I can't say it felt physical. It was almost a reality illusion. In fact, the state of being then was more of a dream illusion, something like how the Buddhists define the experience of existence. The procedures of psychic surgery came to mind. The psychic surgeons claim they are working only on the auras of the body anyway, and the body is nothing but coagulated thought substantiated by the physical in our third-dimension reality. The priest practitioners separated the left side of my brain (male) from the right side (female) and proceeded to divide my ethereal body in half, right down the middle. It was not frightening but more a divine recollection of what both halves of me had been before I had a body . . . in other words, two perfectly balanced conglomerated sparks of God.

I was now half of my former self—whatever "self" meant—and immediately I felt lonely. More than lonely, I felt the need to struggle to unite again with my other half. Since I didn't know how to unite, because I had never been separated, I realized I had to develop a technique for reamalgamation. I saw others around me going through the same lonely struggle. But we had help. The help has come to be called Tantric practice. In other words, we needed to develop a system of returning to our other half through fusing with another body. Hence—sexual union with another.

Later in our future, perhaps we will learn the reunification of our original selves. For now, learning through struggle and polarity has come into being with all its tragic implications. For me, the decision to submit to sexual division has been the most polarizing, isolating, and disastrous decision in human history. Ever since we agreed to the experiment, we have been looking for our other half: the story of love, sex, and desire on which empires have risen and fallen. All because we have never felt whole, and indeed, separated from the genetic unity that we were originally. The etymology of the word "disaster" is *disastrado,* torn asunder from the astral. When we were originally the astral sparks of God, we were united in ourselves, reflecting the Source of Creation itself. What made us so curious to experience only half of who we are? Did we feel a sense of static bliss that needed disruption in order to learn more about ourselves?

In my view, we chose the most difficult way to evolve and learn. There are many ways to learn—I don't see that "difficult" has to be one of them. Each person's life today has been mainly about the struggle and stickiness of finding a mate who suffices in making us feel whole and understood and recognized. I have come to understand that that mate is me. I am coming to the sage-ing of finding my other half in myself again. I feel more unified, and therefore I believe that is why I am remembering the trials and tribulations of my own ancient history.

# chapter

## 6

DEAR READER, HAVE YOU EVER SEEN YOUR HOUSE CRY?

I have. It started at my ranch house. The pipes leaked everywhere, all over my clothes, shoes, carpets, etc. We couldn't find the problem. Then just after I moved in, my house in Santa Fe, the house from which I write, began to leak. Tiny rivulets of water would frequently run down the walls and drip from the ceilings. I called a plumber. He couldn't find a source. The roofer found no problem. By chance, I ran into an Indian shaman friend of mine, and I described the problem with my leaking house to her.

"You have unexpressed sorrow. The house is crying for you," she said.

The beauty of what she said stunned me, and it made sense to me, too. But what was I suppressing? I have always been an optimistic, cheerful person, rarely ever troubled by depression. I always thought my general outlook was positive because I almost always expressed what I was feeling, whether it was anger, joy, confusion, or anything else.

But it wasn't so simple as that. I was finding as I aged and continued my questioning and searching that that search path was becoming more and more narrow. There were fewer people on the path with me, though I always knew such an adventure had always been characterized as an alone pursuit—not lonely— but alone. Yes, I was finding that regardless of how many others might be on their own paths, I needed to walk alone. What I hadn't bargained for was how full of sorrow I had become over the state of the world and probably hadn't expressed it in an effort to be positive and hopeful about the future. But the physical world around me, my houses, knew what I was feeling.

I began to reflect on my pilgrimage across Spain. The Santiago de Compostela Camino was a pilgrimage taken by many ancient leaders because it put them in personal touch with the sorrows of the human race and therefore pointed them toward how that state of being could be improved. To touch sorrow was to find leadership and change. It was true that for me the real Camino began after I finished the Santiago de Compostela Camino.

Perhaps my leaking houses were acting as a mirror for what I should allow myself to do.

I went downstairs and stood under a leak in the dining room and looked up, allowing the "house tears" to lightly fall on my face. I let my mind go to where it desired to be. Soon I felt so clutched with sorrow that it alarmed me. I knew I had been feeling discouraged with us as a human race, but now, in this moment, I allowed myself to feel viscerally what we had done to ourselves. In fact, I wondered how I could live with this feeling. It wasn't so much about what we were doing to one another. It was about the trees and birds and animals and bumblebees. We had become so cruel to our living environment. I found myself sobbing under the leak. The house's tears mingled with mine. It was a moment I'll never forget.

Then I began to allow some of the truths I was afraid of, but hadn't really admitted, to begin to seep into my awareness. Compared to the disasters occurring in the world, they were, of course, trivial, but they were still parts of my daily life that I had been reluctant to acknowledge.

For example, I don't like to drive at night anymore. The landmarks seem unfamiliar, and I feel lost. For me that is a terrible feeling. I thought of all the people in the world who were rudderless and without landmarks of their own and without light. I recognized the unacknowledged fear I must have for where we are headed as human beings, and I realized I had unacknowledged fear about quite a few things. And it was making me sad. But I wasn't crying. My house was.

Did I have a fear of growing old even though I seemed to find it quite enjoyable?

I remembered a cold, foggy night in particular. I had gone to the grocery store and bought small portions of food, enough to feed only myself. *Only myself,* I thought with a chill. And would that be the case for the rest of my life? Would I really live and die alone?

Then, as I allowed my consciousness to continue to wander, the future seemed like the past and the past the future. The present was both to me. I remembered dying before. It was like a birth. It was light and without loneliness. Dying was a new beginning.

As I stood there with the water droplets falling on me, I was aware of a "presence" around me—very comforting and friendly, almost spurring me on to touch other unacknowledged truths.

Suddenly I was in a deep swimming pool as a child, afraid that I would drown because I couldn't get to the top in time to breathe. I began to cough and retch under the leaking pipes as I remembered really dying in another time and place (probably Atlantis sinking . . .) Then—the rebirth and the light . . . nothing really to fear.

I felt I was having a life review. I remembered the time my dad almost drove the car off a bridge and into a river when a draw-bridge went up. He had been drinking and the rest of the family was screaming in fear . . . Morgantown, Maryland. I'll never forget the name of the town. I wondered how people who have had truly harrowing experiences ever get over them. What do they do with their minds and their memories? For those living in apocalyptic circumstances, I can only imagine how sorrowful it must be. I am assuaged only by remembering the real meaning of the word "apocalypse": It comes from the Greek work *apokalipsis* meaning "to disclose or reveal."

Soon after my time under the leaking pipes, the leaking stopped—in both houses. I can't give a rational, scientific explanation. Neither the houses nor I am crying now. But another time will come. I'm grateful to the tears of my houses for mirroring what I couldn't acknowledge. They offered a unique window into my consciousness, helping me to become more fully aware of my thoughts and feelings.

We live in such a mechanistic world that most people regard consciousness as irrelevant. In speaking to Dr. Larry Dossey about healing beyond the body, he makes the point that we can't heal the body without attending to the consciousness of the individual. He says a more positive consciousness heals, and we must learn the difference between brain and mind. We know where the brain is located, but the mind is somewhere in space and time. The brain operates on its own; the mind is tied and connected with the "all."

Doctors have long lists of events they can't explain where the consciousness of their patients is concerned. But doctors and nurses have a hierarchy to uphold. Their medical training is strict and limited. The "unlimitedness" of healing would be frowned upon in their circles.

Great creative genius is often "cured" by Prozac and antipsychotic drugs if the genial person is antisocial or marches to his or her own drummer. An "out of the mainstream" journey, regardless of the profession, has to be courageous. Those people live and function in other dimensions, and often their creativity is killed off by conventional thinking. Part of our creative spark is being a little "nuts." Thought comes from an infinite reservoir. The brain is the channeler for the mind and creativity, and some people say the brain is not at all involved with their creativity. "It just comes to me," they'll say. Sometimes through a feeling, a vision, a dream . . . whatever. . . . We tap into the all—the "other." And everyone has direct access to that "all." I have been healed by it.

I want to have access to the "all" and because of that, sometimes I feel pressured and isolated by the constrictions of conventional thinking. But I like living on the edge of thought. Some of my friends say I have an active imagination. I don't feel it's my "imagination." But again I say, I agree with Einstein: "Imagination is more important than knowledge or information."

I don't like boundaries of thought. It's ridiculous. I'm finding a place of comfort on the edge. Our actions create reactions, and I'm willing to live with them. Sometimes it's not comfortable. I'm prepared to accept that a conventional culture will reject some of my "imaginings." But there are equal discomforts in being conventional!

I remember learning in school that the Greeks encouraged dreaming because out of those dreams came diagnoses and cures. Most doctors and leaders in alternative fields say they dream therapies and cures because they are tapped into the universal knowledge of ALL, and when they surrender to it, they learn and creatively invent.

Since we are basically living in a holographic state of being, there is no linear "time," really. Einstein said we are not linear beings. So we have access to the past and the present and the future. We think we live in a linear world, but that is the limitation of conventional thinking. Stephen Hawking talks about it during his seminars and lectures: "We are basically living in an illusion of linear reality," he says. "But life is really an illusion." That is why dreams are so valuable. They are nonlinear because we are non-linear. Science is now confirming this reality.

So nonlinear consciousness influences what we think is real. That is what has happened to me. As an actor and artist, when I am really into the moment, that is all there is. I have no sense of past or future—they are included in the now. It feels like I tap into the creativity of everything and I am not even the one doing the acting. It is an awesome "forgetfulness of oneself." It feels like I become an instrument of expression, but I can't say that I'm expressing myself. I'm expressing something grander and older and more majestic than the self I am aware of.

I believe this is why art lasts beyond limited thinking. Cyril Connelly said, "Art is man's attempt to preserve his imagination against time." The artist feels holographic when creating. That is why I ask so many questions about the nature of reality. I need to understand what reality truly is. This is what quantum physics is attempting to prove. We affect our own reality simply by the way we look at it. The observed is altered by the observer. The observer (us) is a holographic spiritual being with innate and unrecognized power of the all.

"Know thyself and that truth will set you free," is the challenge. We will not have a coexistence of science and spirituality until we understand that all minds come together to make up the universal mind. This is what Hawking and Einstein and great artists are talking about. It is impossible to be separated from anything or anyone else. We are all basically one mind, one consciousness. If we weren't so mechanistic about our bodies, we would feel the "one mind of all" more acutely.

We are so attached to our bodies that it creates tension and fear. Because we are so invested in our physical bodies, we often become depressed with a kind of free-flowing hostility about ourselves. We become afraid that there is never enough time to do what we "think" we need to do. We get headaches, body aches, and stomachaches . . . the negativity in our bodies hurts everything around us . . . even the water we drink—because our consciousness and the consciousness of water are all one. The famous experiments with "happiness-infused" water as opposed to water that has been influenced with negativity and depression are startling. Plants watered with positive water thrived . . . negative water caused the plants to die.

I have interviewed Cleve Backster about his book *Primary Perception: Biocommunication with Plants, Living Foods and Human Cells.* Backster's work was included in Peter Tompkins and Christopher Bird's book *The Secret Life of Plants* and another book, *The Secret Life of Your Cells.*

Backster used to work for and with the CIA and headed up their polygraph division, so he was well schooled in the science of biocommunication and electrical responses in people. Later, he carried his knowledge of this field into studies involving plant life, trees, and even to the cellular level in other living organisms. His experiments were fascinating. He showed that despite their lack of a nervous system, plants are sentient life forms that sense, and respond to, external events. This can be observed by using a polygraph machine to measure changes in the plant's conductivity and vibrational energy, much as a polygraph can detect similar changes in humans. Backster found that if he held a match close to a plant, the electrical response in the plant was similar to that of a human experiencing fear. Then he found that all he had to do was *think* about lighting the match, and the plant would respond with fear. More recently, he has discovered that plants and trees in the Middle East are reacting with fear to the terrorism and war around them.

The plants he has worked with respond to negativity and caring with equal negative and positive emotion. They can experience fear or happiness. Plants and trees have memory.

When he went about cracking open a dozen eggs he found the fear reaction in the first egg caused the other eggs to seemingly "faint" so they wouldn't feel the pain. Yogurt reacted in terror when penicillin was injected to kill unwanted bacteria.

But to me the most exciting conclusions Backster and others found was that all sentient life immediately reacted to the thought and intention of an act long before the act itself. In other words, all consciousness is connected, not separate from itself and others.

In the sixties, when nearly everyone was experimenting with drugs, my friends explained how they loved being high because they could see the possibility of joy and love, etc. It has been proven that liquor and drugs dull and block out the lower energy senses that we suffer from and allow us to experience the higher levels of who we can be—and really are. We can then become addicted to the higher experience. But what about the lower fears—shame, anxiety, anger, etc.—the demons that we fight in ourselves and others. If our consciousness started inside of us, at home, perhaps we wouldn't go abroad and fight wars. It's an amazing revelation to realize that the defects we see in others are more about the defects we can't abide in ourselves. I have trouble with impatient people because I am so impatient myself. My impatience then leads to so many other things. People who are slow-minded and insist on denying the obvious drive me to distraction. I loathe clichés in others because I'm afraid of being cliché myself. I regard the use of clichés as indications of a lazy mind. Clichés are a simplification of a more complicated truth, even if I do resort to them from time to time.

To play a part exactly the way it is written is cliché. There is a contradictory underbelly to everything and everyone. That's what I'm interested in. On the other hand, clichés save a lot of time and energy. So since I'm so impatient, I should be grateful for them. There's the contradictory underbelly in me.

Many people who are interested in expanding their consciousness use drugs . . . the Timothy Leary approach. Yet our legal system puts millions of people behind bars every year for trying to block out lower energy senses and find the higher potential. Why doesn't our legal system teach rehabilitation through meditation and prayer so the people who are addicted to drugs and alcohol can find their higher power another way?

Human history is replete with the struggle of human beings attempting to comprehend the Great Truth, while the System finds a way to deflate that search in favor of the Church and State, which almost always leads to institutionalized war. Stay within the System, and you're guaranteed to have to kill either yourself or someone else.

How about becoming the change we wish to see?

Whether we are philosophers, politicians, scientists, artists, mathematicians, or work in a factory sharpening pencils, our questions in life all converge at the same place: Who are we and what is the nature of our consciousness?

Each of us is a computer of information that we haven't yet learned to access. Who fed the info into the computer? We did. Our consciousness bridges all species—maybe even computers. I know that when I'm in a bad mood the computer in my TV satellite dish crashes. And on top of that, my car won't start. The only time the chandelier in *Phantom of the Opera* didn't work was when I was in the audience. I was in a foul mood, and I'm surprised it didn't fall on me. I have heard of computer empaths being kept on duty because they have the talent to communicate with the computer to restore its function. In other words, even computers respond to human thought. The right people have a therapeutic effect on computers just by walking into the room. Others can aggressively stop the functioning of huge machines. Everything responds to human consciousness: nature, animals, people, and machines. It would be important to the human race if we each made an effort to have our consciousness become a more healing presence.

And where did our consciousness come from? What is the source of our unrealized power?

I believe that everyone's behavior in life is accountable to the universe, and we are all connected to what Jung called "the collective unconscious." We have the capacity to "know" virtually anything the moment we ask for it. There isn't a question that we can ask for which there isn't an available answer. The universe is very cooperative. It is happy to oblige us if for no other reason than it is happy we recognized its existence.

Who we become and what we are is determined by our perceptions. And our perceptions are a result of our beliefs, the choices we make, and what we want as our goals. We have what Dr. David Hawkins calls "Paradigm Blindness." We can't relate to something that hasn't been defined in a context that we understand or have been educated to. We are unable to see or recognize an event until we have a definition or a context with which to identify it.

The natives on the islands of Hawaii couldn't see the ships of Magellan, sails and all, because they had never been there before. The shamans saw the ships because they lived in a more expanded reality. They described and defined what the ships looked like. The more limited the parameters of consciousness, the more constrained the experience of life. Without consciousness there is no way to experience who we are.

And human-ness is only one way to experience who we are. The more limited our sense of self, the smaller our life seems. If we expanded our sense of self, the more expansive our lives would become. That is why meditation is so useful. We go into the expanded inner universe of ourselves when we learn to let go of our goals, fears, and education. We only need to experience what we already know. That is what is meant by self-realization.

When I look at the outside stimuli of young people nowadays, it is horrifying to me. They are being educated about violence by video games, specialized TV, the world news, and behavior on the freeways.

Subtle grades of depression are setting in. Depression kills more people in the world than all the diseases combined. So what are we doing with our civilization? Our rules of church-defined good and evil are electing our leaders and sustaining an ongoing state of absolutism without regard for another point of view. Our conventional morality is programming our citizens into a dumbed-down state of being, which is the fuel for a velvet fascism.

How can we recognize the difference between truth and falsity in our state of being? The Buddhists say we are "trapped in a dream" and "humanity is an affliction" that we should no longer be burdened with. We are fully responsible and accountable for what we've become. It's time to pay the piper.

Perhaps we simply need to have compassion for each other's blindness so that the paradigm blindness can shift. We can no longer feel comfortably dumbed-down in our self-imposed ignorance. It's time to wake up to the uncomfortableness of who we are and always have been.

I love my books and my library, but there are other sources of information that I tap into, and they reveal truths that I haven't found in my books. I have long been an advocate of trance channeling if I feel the instrument (the channeler) is pure in intent and can keep his or her own personal opinions out of the information that comes through. It is imperative that the channeler have no attachment to the outcome or the effect of the information.

Edgar Cayce was a trance channeler and a highly respected one because most of his information was useful and accurate. He and others (Kevin Ryerson, for example) channeled information on health, welfare, and the pursuit of happiness. They seem to be in accord with the universal consciousness and, indeed, most of their information relates to the ups and downs of human consciousness. They have the ability to set aside their own level of consciousness to allow spiritual information to come through. Some say Cayce channeled his own superconsciousness (or higher self) rather than a separate spiritual being.

Under hypnosis, anyone can touch the creative component of themselves that lies in their superconscious and their subconscious. Carl Jung said that the collective unconscious is where the real truth lies. The word "entity" simply means being of energy—a nonphysical intelligence. So channelers such as Kevin Ryerson act as a "radio" medium so that these "entity teachers" can bring us knowledge from the vast reservoirs of "heavenly" information. Some have had physical incarnations; some have not. But all of them seem to have no judgment in what they impart and teach.

Since the turn of the millennium, energy itself has speeded up. Everyone feels it. And science now tells us that *everything* is a question of energy . . . physical and nonphysical. The frequency of energy is the new science; therefore, the world of science has, admittedly or not, entered the sphere of the frequency of spirit.

When a gifted psychic holds an ancient pottery shard, he or she can "intuit," "feel," determine by energy frequency its relative age. This is called psychometry and is becoming more and more useful in determining the original history of our evolution. The truth lies not just in the physical but in the energy frequency of the physical. And matter itself is speeding up its frequency as though it wants to be recognized for what it truly is. Magnetic resonance exposes the secrets of time and dates. As someone once said, "Time is what the gods invented to keep everything from happening at once."

The memory of all the collective unconscious and supercon-scious for all sentient beings is stored in what is called the "Akashic Records." Nothing is lost to time. All still exists and is therefore accessible to those who are psychically talented in these areas. I'm not sure how to define "psychically talented." I only know it when I feel it. Then I no longer believe it—I *know* it. We are leaving the age of belief now and are entering the age of knowing.

We have forgotten our ancient spiritual technology and are finding it again. In fact, the spiritual base is that from which all other technology flows. We are remembering what we once "knew."

Humans used to see patterns of energy. I remember it. We saw human auras (halos) and knew how to heal with the vibrational frequency of color. Gemstones (rubies, emeralds, sapphires, etc.) are valuable today because our ancient memory remembers they were colorful healing stones. We had, in ancient times, a high level of awareness to invent and monitor spiritual technology. Our cities sprang up around high-frequency merid-ian ley lines.

We had an extremely high level of spiritual culture dating from Atlantis, Lemuria, Sumeria, and Egypt. I remember that time, too. I like very much to relax, put the turmoil of my consciousness today aside, and go back to the times when I *know* I lived in those ancient civilizations during my soul's journey through time. Can I prove something I believe? No. But I can find confidence and even educational entertainment in something I *know*.

There are about 70 million of us so-called cultural creatives in the United States alone and another 70 million in Europe. We revere nature and life and God above all else. We want to live in our memories of advanced understanding of those three elements. I, and others, remember that when Atlantis sank, we slowly began to lose our psychic sciences and the awareness of the science of our soul's journey. It is, I believe, now essential that we regain our soul's purpose and the memory of why we are here. We need to cope with our anxieties with a spiritually developing culture.

It is clear that we are killing one another over religion. It is high time we tried spirituality, which I believe religion was intended to be in the first place. I believe we are the repository of a vast body of knowledge that even supersedes our ability to cope with it. That is why so much of it is ridiculed and mocked. But a flat world was easier to cope with than a round one. It was easier to cope with our one world which the sun revolved around alone in the universe than what seems to be slowly transpiring as multispecied world universes which revolve around billions of suns. It is time to wake up to the knowledge we've forgotten we possess and understand that each of us has a function in a gazillion-person band of spirits.

We need to remind ourselves of the architecture of our brains and what profound knowledge has been transferred there from our soul's journey. We know EVERYTHING. The task is to live in a nonlinear way so we'll remember we are all one and all part of the creative source.

That brings me to a subject that I'm trying especially hard to understand these days. If there is a malevolent force in the world, what is it? Do we create that force in order to learn from it? And is that force an unresolved energy of anger, or fear, or whatever, from a previous lifetime that remains alive until we recognize it and work through it? Are the demons that rattle around in our own hearts really memories of what went before and the debt that hasn't been forgiven?

According to statistics and research, 9 million Americans harbor negative thoughts toward others. And 5 percent actually pray for harm to come to others. It would be good for those people to be aware of the laws of karma . . . what one puts out will come back to the sender. It's the law of the universe . . . the law of One.

I think we demonize others because we see the demons in ourselves. But are we inherently and intrinsically hardwired to act atrociously? Jung calls it "the repression of the shadows." What nasty habits we all have! The *repression* of our shadows denies that we can be nasty. If we don't look at those tendencies, we can be vulnerable to manipulation. And God knows, all humans are victims of, and vulnerable to, manipulation. I've always wondered what the source of our darkness is. It's not enough to say evil. I've never heard a good definition of evil, anyway. I've never heard a good definition of love either, for that matter. One person's love is another person's affliction. So where did our Earth-plane morality come from? There seems to be a more ethical morality on higher dimensions. Or is that true? Does the ultimate God have a polarity of good and evil? We know that opposites attract, each providing juice for the other, but does the Divine Source need that kind of polarity, too? Or is the Divine Source total love?

We know that peace is the opposite of chaos, but do we need one to know the other? Does that mean we are forever doomed to the shadows in order to see the light *and* vice versa?

Do we, as human beings, need to be wounded warriors ourselves in order to heal ourselves and others? And are we born with a sense of reason, or is reason something we learn? We actors often sit around and talk about these things because we try to determine where our talent comes from. We would also like to know the meaning of "star quality"!

A related and perhaps more important question I ask myself is, "From what source did human *negativity* spring?" This question has been the basis for much of my searching—and "the Devil made me do it" isn't good enough. I will try to explain simply what I have uncovered up to now.

First, negativity is described as various intertwined human "beliefs" emanating from many sources: the Devil, Lucifer, whatever, to name a few. But what makes the most sense to me is the following.

In the most ancient of times, we were each part of the God consciousness: one mind, many thoughts, each of us being a thought to God. All souls were cocreators with God (the source of all life). We created life with the God spark. As we became more and more enamored of our physical cocreated creations, we began to invest our interest and identities with them. So attracted were we to the physicality of what we had created that we slowly lost our awareness of our own divine nature. We began to identify ourselves purely with the material plane until we incarnated into our creations. Thus the description that we had become "fallen angels." In fact we had "incarnated" our souls into the physical beings we had created because all angels and souls have free will.

A wave of angels who had witnessed our total identification with the physical and material plane elected to come to our rescue because we had developed a kind of divine amnesia. Their plan was that in order to further our evolution of consciousness, in which we could reclaim our awareness of our divinity, we should undergo a duration of time on the material plane in order to see the polarity between the material self and the divine self. This approach proved to be a mistake because it was a self-organizing approach, devoid of the inclusion of the divine, and revolved entirely around the material. Therefore it was less of an evolution of the divine in mankind and more a celebration of the material. According to Edgar Cayce and Judeo-Christian mysticism, the leader of the rescue angels was Lucifer. The name Lucifer means light bearer. He and his soul group were less prepared for incarnation into the physical than those who preceded them. They effectively became "trapped" in the physical, becoming another wave of "fallen angels." Lucifer's original position as an archangel in the Divine Order was one of "humanity's caretaker." After becoming trapped in the physical incarnation, he became humanity's accuser. The word "Satan" means the "adversary" or the "accuser." Lucifer/Satan held humanity accountable only to the standards of karma (cause and effect), not to the standards of the Divine Forgiveness. Thus humanity was held to suffer the laws of karmic prophecy—thus the works of the Devil. Was this the origin of the negativity on Earth and the origin of the myths of the "fallen angels"?

The Luciferian "fallen angels" taught that the original physically incarnated souls should go through karmically bound Earth-plane lessons and experience, traveling through as many cycles of incarnation necessary to understand their divinity. Thus there developed a duality and struggle between the original souls, who now identified strictly with the material Earth-plane matter (the negative), and the angel beings of energy and light, who had a purpose of teaching divinity on Earth but did it in a mistaken manner. Free will is the opportunity to choose the wrong course of action on the way back to God.

We have since come to understand that we are not physical beings desiring to be spiritual. We are spiritual beings here only to explore the meaning of cocreation in the physical.

As a scientist and an astronaut, Dr. Edgar Mitchell may seem an unlikely person to have information about this kind of subject matter, but his own experiences, which he and I have discussed on several occasions, are truly astounding. Ed was the sixth man who went to the moon. He traveled some 5 million miles on his journey, but the journey through himself was the most awe-inspiring. Ed is a friend of mine. I met with him nearly every day when I was shooting *In Her Shoes* in Florida, where he lives. He was comfortable describing his soul-expanding experience. We talked about René Descartes, the great thinker in the 1600s. Descartes was a cardinal in the church (a Prince of the Church, in fact), a mathematician, and a philosopher. He came to the conclusion that body, mind, and spirit are each a separate realm of reality. Essentially, his conclusions were reached in order to tone down the Inquisition so that intellectuals could proceed with their analysis without so much fear and interference. Of course, they could do that as long as they stayed away from the mind and spirituality.

Ed feels we have built Western science around that premise and still regard spirituality and physicality as separate in mankind with no influence on each other. However, we are now beginning to learn that they profoundly interact with each other. A physicist would say: "If you want to understand the human condition, you must first understand the universe." A mystic would say: "If you want to understand the universe, you must first understand the self."

As Ed sees it, they are both right because we live in a participatory, interactive, self-organizing universe. So we are looking at two faces of the same reality. He told me about the epiphany he had while traveling back to Earth from the moon. Because of the lack of atmosphere, he saw the world and surrounding galaxy ten times brighter than from any vantage point on Earth. He described his feelings as he saw our tiny Earth like a small ball floating in front of him, surrounded by the magnificent stars and galaxies and galaxy clusters. He said he felt the molecules in his own body. He felt the molecules in the spacecraft itself as well as the molecules of his partners. He said all the molecules seemed to be manufactured from some ancient generation of stars. He was awestruck by the deep, personal, inner revelation he experienced. "Everything and everyone was interconnected in a mysterious way. It was ecstasy . . . truly. I'll never forget it," he said. "It changed me forever. Now physics is explaining it in terms of the quantum hologram."

He went on to explain the aftermath. He began questioning himself. He talked to other astronauts who had had the same experience but were reluctant to discuss it. The insight he received produced a profound shock to his system. This magnificent ecstasy was inexplicable to him. Why does it happen that way? It was so powerful he has spent his life since trying to figure it out. He founded the Institute for Noetic Sciences, whose name was taken from the Greek word "*noe*," meaning higher consciousness. He authored a book, *Psychic Exploration—A Challenge for Science*. He said his experience was so powerful that it has motivated his life ever since. He said he has been trying to reconcile his science (as a test pilot, etc.) with his religious training. "We live in an enormous cosmos," he said, "and we are only beginning to understand and realize its meaning. The scientists are now seriously questioning the Big Bang theory."

I mentioned that Dr. Stephen Hawking (who occupies the Sir Isaac Newton Chair at Cambridge University in England) had told me the universe never had a beginning or an end. He said, "To come to one of my lectures would be the same as attending a Buddhist lecture. We are saying the same thing." He went on to tell me that "anyone who says I don't believe in God has not heard what I'm saying."

When I asked Ed if he believed in God, he said, "Well, I try to talk in scientific lingo, but my research tells me that an inner mystical core is where 'God' is. When we try to create an explanation, we have to do it in acceptable cultural terms. Those cultural terms are rigid in practice and structure. Talk to the great mystics of any culture, and they are all talking about the same inner experience but in their own cultural and even peculiar language. The fact is that this inner-marking core ecstasy is common to all people and is worthy of scientific investigation. For now, we call it all myth. Anyway, at the bottom of everything is ENERGY. And energy carries information. But the startling thing is that that information is nonlocal. I know that's a scientific word, but let me explain. Nonlocality to a physicist is what interconnectedness is to a mystic. They're the same!"

I asked him if he thought *all* information was stored somewhere. He said yes, because all nonlocality information is available. We just don't know *how* it's stored. "This could explain what the mystics call the Akashic Records and how great seers like Edgar Cayce can access it. But one has to let go of the ego to do it. That's not easy when you're caught up in left-brain science."

"We need the scientific tape removed from our eyes so we can truly see?"

"Yes, and remember, it's an evolutionary progressive universe. We make progress slowly but we do make it. We need to realize the God power within. We live in a physical and spiritual interactive system. This is what I'm trying to prove. We affect 'reality' and have to react to the 'reality' that's already there. It requires a paradigm shift in thinking."

"So do we, in effect, create our own reality, like the hackneyed phrase says?"

"Well, if we concentrate on the Divine within rather than concentrate on the God without, we're much closer to what's really happening."

Ed went on to tell me that he meditates "fastidiously" every day. He said he was trying to balance the polarities of what the Asians call "polarity of pain and pleasure, happiness and sorrow, male and female, and the energies of yin and yang." He said through meditation he could reproduce the epiphany he had in the spacecraft. "Meditation is a way of being. It's no good with drugs and other chemicals. Your whole life changes when you meditate regularly. But this is what the mystics have been telling us for eons."

I asked him if he asked for answers to his quantum hologram questions during meditation. He said yes. When I asked how he heard the answers, he said, "Some people hear the answers, some see visions. My particular mode is symbiance. It *feels* right. And the answer comes from a heart place, not from the mind or brain. It's a knowing, followed by a sensation of the body. It is a sensitivity to the receptors of the body, and that's where nonlocality comes in."

I described seeing the meditating monks sitting in deep snow and ice in the Himalayas. I saw them actually melt the snow and ice around them.

"The grand universe within meets the grand universe without," said Ed. "We have to put them in harmony. 'Meaning' comes from within. Meaning is a part of consciousness. There is no meaning to information. We need to learn to give meaning to information because otherwise information is just patterns of energy. Meaning is where we come in."

I thought for a moment, then I decided to ask him something that had been underneath all of my searching and questioning about consciousness and God. I just blurted it out, since he was a mystical astronaut. "Ed," I asked, "do extraterrestrials have meaning?"

He didn't seem shocked, rather almost grateful I had brought it up. "Well," he said after a long pause and a smile, "there is very strong evidence that they are here, and we are being visited."

# chapter

# 7

I'M GAZING OUT AT THE NIGHT SKY, APPRECIATING THAT I LIVE in New Mexico. Is this, as some say, the backyard of extraterrestrial intelligence? I can remember myself as a child looking through my telescope at the same night sky. I have long since dispensed with the concern of being ridiculed over my belief in star visitors. I've always known they are there. Besides, there is simply too much evidence to dismiss from witnesses and from those who have not only been contacted but abducted as well.

I walk back inside to my library and peruse my books and pictures again. From what I've learned and read, apparently the star visitors deeply want to be acknowledged so that they can be helpful to us in our chaotic and vastly disturbing state of being on Earth. Without our acknowledgment of them, they would be guilty of karmic interference. The material I have gleaned is astonishing, sometimes confusing, but surely rewarding. It comes from many sources: contactees (people who have had contact directly or subliminally, or have willingly gone aboard a craft); abductees (people who have been taken aboard a craft without their consent); and doctors and psychologists who believe the stories of star visitations and work with their patients accordingly.

I have seen (along with other people I was with) many crafts in the skies of Peru and Mexico, but I've never had the experience at my own ranch, as have many others who have been there. In fact, each residence I've ever occupied has produced star visitor phenomena for people visiting me, but never for me—I've always been away at the time. The lives of some of my friends have been changed due to what they witnessed, but star visitors are judicious in choosing those whom they trust with the experience. So I always ask—why not me, too?

I assuage my disappointment with the understanding that I would willingly get on the craft and leave. I suppose I'm meant to stay here and report on their presence and phenomena.

Many realities are difficult for our Western culture to accept. We have a materialistic and mechanistic worldview. We have a vested interest in scientifically proving a considered reality before we can accept it. We separate the spiritual from the physical, and we have made that gulf inviolate.

We don't accept that there might be unseen realities as powerful as those we can thump on. To me, the absence of evidence is not the evidence of absence. We do not know what to do with a phenomenon that crosses the provability barrier. I'm the kind of person who listens to my own truth—but it is not without an objective perusal before I count it as real to me. I don't like close-mindedness in myself or anyone else. I very much admire imagination and, yes, I do believe we each create our own reality, probably according to what we need to learn.

I feel that a paradigm shift in consciousness is in play. We certainly need it. It is time to open up to the reality of other dimensions and the inner power that we are capable of. I believe we are citizens in a cosmos of intelligent beings. We are not alone and never have been. And we are not the preeminent beings in a universe that we know very little about. In fact, it appears that we live in a universe that is quite different from the one we have been taught to believe in.

Our life here on Earth is profoundly threatened, and we feel that every day. What will the journey to our future be, then, if we have no help? If we suspend our ego-driven belief that we are the center of cosmic life in the universe, perhaps we will find that there is a connecting principle, a caring link that we have, not only to each other on Earth but to cosmic intelligent beings that we sense but somehow can't prove are there. We seem to be afraid to consider seriously the truth of this. It would profoundly shatter the belief we have in our religions, institutions, and even our sanity. The question then becomes one not of shattering our reality but one of examining our FEAR.

*Why are we really afraid?* Why do we think the notion of celestial travelers is a ridiculous or scary one? It is here in America that the fear and ridicule are the most prevalent. Not so in Russia, China, South America, and most of all, Mexico. I will get into the star beings visitations in other countries later, but I believe one of the reasons for our close-minded policies involves maintaining the need for the military-industrial complex. The good news is that many of those in military intelligence and in undercover intelligence groups who are now senior citizens are rethinking the security oaths they took long ago. Some are beginning to divulge what they have kept secret during their lifetimes up until now.

Most Americans don't believe our government is telling the truth about Unidentified Flying Objects anyway. Whatever the consequences, we need to know the truth so that we can determine how to participate in our own future in a world that is suffering from such violence, chaos, and disharmony. We need to become enlightened about life in the cosmos so that we can determine our role and behavior in full knowledge of the truth.

We've lived long enough with conspiracy theories and the fear of clandestine organizations and "shadow governments." For too long we have felt the systematic cover-up that denies E.T. presence. Too many people have had experiences that attest to another reality.

*Disinformation* has become a sophisticated tactic to divert energy and information away from those who have had experiences, resulting in those people suffering from feelings of insanity. I know the feeling because much of my public interest in such issues has obviously caused many people to call me wacky. But now curiosity about these issues has entered the mainstream and it seems obvious to many that the burden of proof has purposely been placed on groups that incurred the ridicule of the media. Military intelligence has used the media to brand UFO researchers kooks and paranoid, which obviously makes it easier to disregard them. I am not a believer. I am an "open-minder." Perhaps I am playing hide-and-seek with pragmatic reality. But the truth seems to hide as much as we seek to find it. I have come to feel that the truth is hiding in plain sight.

Official military intelligence policy has been to maintain secrecy of the star visitor presence in any way necessary . . . intimidation, theft of personal documents, destruction of bank accounts, financial ruin, public humiliation, and enforced oaths of secrecy. The secrecy oath that military intelligence people take is called "Oath Upon Inadvertent Exposure to Classified Security

Data or Information." The consequence of taking the oath is the signing away of constitutional rights. If the security agreement is violated, there is no trial, no right of appeal, and the person is sentenced to a federal penitentiary for twenty years. This is usually enough to maintain secrecy, though there have been some who have violated the oath. The practice of cover-up has itself become so sophisticated that the accusation of cover-up *is* the cover-up.

A prominent Pentagon official, Col. Philip Corso, who served in the Eisenhower administration and later headed the Foreign Technology desk in the Army's Research & Development department, publicly revealed in his 1997 book, *The Day After Roswell*, that he led a top secret, clandestine project to reverse engineer E.T. technology recovered from the Roswell, New Mexico, crash. Out of that came fiber optics, integrated circuit chips, night-vision equipment, and super-tenacity fibers that were made into body armor.

Colonel Corso worked with Lt. Gen. Arthur Trudeau in military intelligence for twenty years, and buried in his office at the Pentagon were the military's most closely guarded secrets: the Roswell, New Mexico, files, the cache of debris and information an Army retrieval team from 509th Army Air Field pulled out of the wreckage of a flying disk that had crashed outside of Roswell, New Mexico, during the first week of July 1947. According to Corso and Trudeau there were two beings in the craft, described as having small, wiry, trim bodies with eyes that looked like wrap-around goggles, who communicated telepathically in English with the humans who found them. One was shot, apparently by a law enforcement officer from Roswell, but the other lived for a time.

Several sources report that soon after the Roswell crash in 1947, President Truman issued an executive order to a top-secret committee called Majestic Twelve to investigate the nature of the flying disks and their occupants and to collect all information about encounters with these phenomena. Originally formed in 1942, Majestic Twelve was primarily interested in techniques of mind control. After Roswell, the group also addressed itself to "Inter-Planetary Phenomenon." It was embedded in Army Intelligence and was said to contain a report by Albert Einstein and Max Oppenheimer on potential relations with E.T. races. This operation has progressed amid complete secrecy for more than fifty years.

According to sources, the working group of Majestic Twelve supposedly included: Central Intelligence director Admiral Roscoe Hillenkoetter; Secretary of Defense James Forrestal; Lieutenant General Nathan Twining of the A.A.F. and then U.S.A.F. Air Material Command; Professor Donald Menzel, Harvard astronomer and Naval Intelligence cryptography expert; Vannevar Bush, Joint Research and Development Board Chairman; Detlev Bronk, chairman of the National Research Council and biologist, who would ultimately be named to the national Advisory Committee on Aeronautics; General Robert Montague, who was General Twining's classmate at West Point, commandant of Fort Bliss with operational control over the command at White Sands; Gordon Gray, President Truman's secretary of the army and chairman of the CIA's Psychological Strategy Board; Sidney Sauers, director of the National Security Council; General Hoyt Vandenberg, Central Intelligence group director prior to Roscoe Hillenkoetter and the U.S.A.F. chief of staff in 1948; Jerome Hunsaker, aircraft engineer and director of the National Advisory Committee on Aeronautics; Lloyd Berkner, member of the Joint Research and Development Board. This was Majestic Twelve, and later at the Eisenhower White House it was simply referred to as "the group."

Apparently, it was General Twining who had carefully orchestrated a complete cover-up of what had happened at Roswell, as well as a full-scale, top-secret military R&D operation to identify the nature of the phenomenon and assess its military threat to the United States.

Reverse engineering of what they retrieved occurred, and from the original group there developed a substructure of loosely confederated committees and subgroups, all kept separate by administrative firewalls so that there would be no information leakage, and also controlled from the top (the White House) and by oaths of secrecy.

UFOs were never referred to as extraterrestrial objects but instead as objects of "foreign technology." Hence, anyone reading the material would consider it innocuous. I began to research Majestic Twelve and soon found myself in a black hole of disinformation. Documents purporting to relate to Majestic Twelve have been hotly debated in the UFO community. The documents I found covered such matters as the conduct to be used when meeting an alien, diagrams and records of tests on UFOs, memos on assorted cover-ups, and descriptions of the president's statements about UFO-related issues. These documents, which contained supposed signatures of important people such as Albert Einstein and Ronald Reagan, created a major debate in the conspiracy and UFO communities, but their authenticity was dubious to me. Some of them, on further investigation, were clearly either fake or planted by someone who wanted them to be true.

I've also spent time investigating some intriguing Canadian documents dating from 1950 and 1951 that were uncovered in 1978. These documents mention the existence of a similar, highly classified UFO study group operating within the Pentagon's U.S. Research and Development Board headed by Dr. Vannevar Bush. Although the name of the group is not given, proponents argue that these documents remain the most compelling evidence that such a group (along the lines of Majestic Twelve) did indeed exist.

Perhaps the most important document ever released in Canada is the Top Secret memo of November 21, 1951, from Wilbert B. Smith, senior radio engineer with the Canadian Department of Transportation. Smith was a highly respected employee, with a master's degree in electrical engineering and several patents to his credit. The memo was sent to the controller of telecommunications and recommended that a research project be set up. "We believe that we are on the track of something which may well prove to be the introduction of a new technology," Smith wrote. "The existence of a different technology is borne out by the investigations which are being carried on at the present time in relation to flying saucers." Smith went on to state that:

A. the matter is the most highly classified subject in the U.S. government, rating higher than the H-bomb;

B. flying saucers exist;

C. their modus operandi is unknown but a concentrated effort is being made by a small group headed by Dr. Vannevar Bush; and

D. the entire matter is considered by the U.S. authorities to be of tremendous significance.

Here was an unarguable link between Vannevar Bush and UFO reverse engineering, similar to what the questionable Majestic Twelve documents describe.

Dear Reader, disinformation is like a black hole that consumes the light of the universe. The light begins with a spark of truth that sails through spiral galaxies of individuals, until the spark is no longer visible, and you are left with only an obscure remembrance of what might have been the truth. I am not even certain that the Wilbert Smith memo is real. It might have been planted.

Books like William Cooper's *Behold a Pale Horse,* Kevin D. Randle's *Case MJ-12,* and Michael E. Salla's *Exopolitics* explored Majestic Twelve and made me more determined to uncover the facts behind the secretive group. I set out on a search for the truth and uncovered a maze. I began at the National Archives and found that there was no record of Majestic Twelve or MJ-12. I went to a friend who was with the FBI and was told that the Bureau had investigated these Majestic Twelve "leaked documents" and the FBI questioned the authenticity of them. FBI personnel then contacted the U.S. Air Force, asking if MJ-12 had ever existed. The Air Force reported that no such group had ever been authorized and had never even been formed. The Bureau's final determination was that the documents were not real.

The more I searched and read, the less substance I found. Yet I felt there was a spark of truth in this vast black hole of disinformation. What is real? Then I realized that those who have had the actual experience are the ones who own the truth.

The documents may be bogus, the claims faulty, and the Majestic Twelve UFO group may be a figment of someone's active imagination, but how does that reconcile with the eyewitness testimony of events? Why would credible people like Corso and Dean and many others step forward in public, open forums and testify that their experiences were real? These people had a great deal at stake and they knew that someone somewhere would attempt to discredit them. Maybe ageing had a role in their taking responsibility for their personal truth and superceded the threat of intimidation. I know the feeling. Perhaps we should be listening to these individuals who report their firsthand experiences instead of relying on "provable" documentation. After all, people are the sparks of truth that bring light to the universe—not government documents.

All material and evidence related to UFO technology is located under research and development on the Foreign Technology desk. There could, therefore, be secret experiments and fiascoes of failed reverse engineering without fear of exposure.

The technology derived from the clandestine reverse engineering of downed craft was shared with IBM, Hughes Aircraft, Bell Labs, and Dow Corning. Despite the repeated governmental denials of reverse engineering from E.T. technology, there are former military, government, and aviation officials who have come forward to share what they know.

In the meantime, Joseph Stalin reportedly had agents on the ground at Alamogordo, New Mexico, who had infiltrated the event at Roswell. When the Americans began to publish cover stories of weather balloons and the like, the Soviets knew the Americans had a real extraterrestrial craft. They had agents at White Sands also; so the Soviets knew as much as we did after the Roswell crash, and the military technological competition came into full tilt. There were spies and counterspies after the retrieval of the Roswell crash. Because of it, I believe the decision was made by

Truman to proceed with a policy of secrecy. He followed much the same course as with the Manhattan Project: It was war, and the information was hidden from the government itself. A new level of security classification was created so that anyone getting information would never have security clearance that comes from the top. There was, therefore, a government within a government, the primary objective being to keep all information regarding E.T.s from the public, except insofar as the media could be manipulated through disinformation and ridicule.

The big question was to become, "Would they ever tell the American people living in an open society what was really going on?"

The military generals opted for complete nondisclosure, but Harry Truman didn't have a military background, and he wasn't so sure, because, as he is supposed to have said to his Central Intelligence "group" director along with the Secretary of Defense, "So what do we do when they land and create more panic in the streets than if we disclosed what we know now?"

My sources tell me that General Twining sent the remains of the crashed aliens, along with the artifacts, to his Air Material Command at Wright Field. Later they went to Fort Bliss, Texas, where General Roger Ramey determined their final disposition. Retired Major Jesse Marcel was the intelligence officer who had been at the crash site. He gave reports to the press that a spacecraft had indeed crash-landed. Later, General Ramey ordered Major Marcel to recant his "flying saucer" story and pose for a news photo with debris from a weather balloon, which he described as the wreckage the retrieval team recovered from outside Roswell. Marcel followed orders and the flying saucer officially became a weather balloon.

The silencing of military witnesses was thorough and from the top. General Ramey treated the incident as a threat to national security and deployed his 509th unit to go into the civilian community, as well as the military, and use any means necessary to suppress the story of the crash and retrieval. No news was allowed to get out, no speculation was to be tolerated, and the story already circulating about a crashed UFO was to be quashed. By the next morning, after the crash, the suppression of the crash story was in full operation. Rancher Mac Brazel, who first said he had been at the site and described the scene, disappeared for two days, then showed up in town driving a new pickup truck, denying he'd ever seen anything. CIC officers turned up at people's houses, ordering them to say, "I didn't see a thing."

The silencing worked well.

The alien bodies had to be autopsied in utmost secrecy and the spacecraft and its contents analyzed, cataloged, and prepared for dissemination to various facilities within the military. The highest security was observed and comments were prepared for credible cover stories. General Twining conducted his operation as if he were in wartime circumstances, under battle conditions. The die was cast: Roswell became Military Intelligence.

In July 2007, a news report appeared that, yet again, calls into question the "official" story of Roswell. It involved Lieutenant Walter Haut, who was the public relations officer at Roswell in 1947—the man who issued the original press releases after the crash. Haut died in 2006, but he left behind a sworn affidavit with instructions that it was to be opened only after his death. Haut's statement asserts that the weather balloon story was just a cover-up. He says he was present at a meeting when pieces of the wreckage were passed around, and he was granted access to the hangar where he saw the craft itself: "It was approx. 12 to 15 feet in length, not quite as wide, about 6 feet high, and more of an egg shape . . . no windows, portholes, wings, tail section, or landing gear were visible." Even more astonishing, in his affidavit he claims to have seen the alien bodies: "Also from a distance, I was able to see a couple of bodies under a canvas tarpaulin. Only the heads extended beyond the covering, and I was not able to make out any features. The heads did appear larger than normal and the contours of the canvas suggested the size of a ten-year-old child."

Haut was often interviewed about the events at Roswell and he never made any such claims during his life. Obviously he was not seeking publicity; more likely he feared being ridiculed for his story. Only after his death would he reveal what he truly experienced that day in July 1947.

Roswell was not the only extrasterrestrial phenomenon Truman had to deal with. I remember being at my childhood home in Arlington, Virginia, in 1952 when across the Potomac River in Washington, D.C., a squadron of UFOs buzzed the Capitol. I had just graduated from high school and was still faithfully peering through my telescope. When I heard the news, it seemed to confirm my convictions that "life out there" existed. I remember seeing Air Force Intelligence Chief Major General John Samford on television a few days later, speaking for President Truman, who guaranteed the American people that the crafts weren't from the Soviet Union, although he couldn't say where they *were* from. I still have a kinescope of that press conference.

It was a Saturday night, July 19, 1952 (I know because I recorded it in my diary). A pilot reported seeing UFOs, two local Air Force bases picked up UFOs, and two Air Force F-94 jets streaked over Washington in hot pursuit. The next morning

the banner headline in *The Washington Post* was SAUCER OUTRAN
JET, PILOT REVEALS. The New York *Daily News:* JETS CHASE D.C. SKY
GHOSTS. The *Washington Daily News:* AERIAL WHATZITS BUZZ WASH-
INGTON D.C. AGAIN.

Indeed, a week later, more UFOs buzzed the White House
and the Capitol, knocking the Korean War and the presidential
campaign off the front pages. *Life* magazine did a cover story
called "There Is a Case for Interplanetary Saucers. Have We
Visitors from Outer Space?" It reviewed ten recent UFO sightings and concluded that they could not be written off as hal-
lucinations, hoaxes, or earthly aircraft. An unnamed Air Force
intelligence officer was quoted saying, "The higher you go in
the Air Force, the more seriously they take the flying saucers."
"Who or what is aboard?" "Where do they come from?" "Why
are they here?" "What are the intentions of the beings who control them?"

There had been lots of publicity since several other sightings had occurred, but the *Life* article was the first time a mainstream magazine had given credence to the theory that UFOs
might really be alien spacecraft. The *Life* story was big news and
covered in more than 350 newspapers across the country. President Truman watched what was happening. The number of UFO
sighting reports to the Air Force went from 23 a month to 82,
to 148. The air controllers watched the UFOs flit across their
screens, then disappear.

Sightings of UFOs and E.T.s after World War II were so
overwhelming in their frequency and scope that the U.S. Air Force
launched three consecutive inquiries. They were called Operation
Sign (1947–1948), Operation Grudge (1948–1952), and Operation Blue Book (1952–1969).

I've read Project Blue Book. It dismissed 12,618 sightings as misidentified aircraft or explainable by natural causes. It left 701 cases as "unidentified." Later the Condon Report, an independent assessment report by the University of Colorado, recommended terminating Project Blue Book. I feel the Condon Report was just another example of a cleverly orchestrated secret government conspiracy to keep the truth hidden from the American public.

A prominent astronomer, Dr. Allen Hynek, served as the astronomical consultant on Grudge and Blue Book between 1949 and 1969. He began as a debunker of UFO phenomena, calling it "a psychological postwar craze." Later, as witnesses and more and more sightings were evident, he changed and became a powerful advocate of the credibility supporting UFO presence. He gave interviews, wrote extensively, and organized scholarly research of the UFO phenomenon as Director of the Center for UFO Studies.

Captain Edward J. Ruppelt was the head of Project Blue Book, the Air Force's official UFO study team. He interviewed a government scientist whom he quoted in his 1956 memoir, *The Report on Unidentified Flying Objects*: "Within the next few days, you're going to have the granddaddy of all UFO sightings. They will occur over Washington or New York—probably Washington."

The UFOs over Washington cruised at a rate of 100 to 130 miles per hour, then abruptly zoomed off in an extraordinary burst of speed. They moved as a cluster, then at other times as individuals. Nobody called Captain Ruppelt, who was out of Washington at the time. He learned about the crafts by reading the newspapers. He called his colleagues to ask who was the expert he should talk to. "You are," they answered. When a reporter finally reached him, he said, "I have no idea what the Air Force is doing. In all probability—nothing."

President Truman was as baffled as everyone else. He asked Major General John Samford, the Air Force's Director of Intelligence, to call a press conference and explain what was happening. Samford's performance could have won an award for bureaucratic doublespeak. He opened with a rambling monologue on the history of UFOs, which he noted dated back to "Biblical times." He mentioned UFO sightings in 1846. When reporters asked about the Washington sightings, he told a story about radar picking up a flock of ducks in Japan in 1950. When asked if controllers had picked up UFO bleeps simultaneously, he speculated about the definition of the word "simultaneously." When asked whether the UFOs were material objects, he speculated on the definition of the word "material." When asked if "qualified" people had seen them, he wondered about the meaning of "qualified." He talked about the crafts being a product of "air and temperature inversion."

Then, in closing, he uttered the following sentence: "That very likely is one that sits apart and says insufficient measurement, insufficient association with other things, insufficient association with other probabilities for it to do any more than to join that group of sightings that we still hold in front of us as saying no."

The reporters wrote that UFOs were caused by Washington's famous "hot air." The reporters knew they'd get more of the same, so they gave up on the story. I had been there for three days, watching the event and the press reaction. After two days there were no more pictures and no more stories. It had been a nonevent.

As I look back on my life, I find the star being connection in my experience to be more than real and, of course, life-generating, in my curiosity as to what is going on even today. I live in the backyard of star beings in New Mexico. I saw evidence of them in Washington, D.C., even though it was successfully covered up in a couple of days. I often ask myself . . . Is this my personal synchronistic destiny at work? Even though I may be ridiculed for revealing my experience and my "enduring" curiosity, I *have* to do it. I cannot stay silent, and I don't believe our military intelligence should either.

We are dealing with spacecraft that have no engines, no fuel, no apparent method of propulsion, peopled with beings who, when encountered, speak in telepathically spiritual terms with much understanding and information about life and destiny. All of them seem superior to us, technologically, regardless of how much they lack in humanity. And yet we have a government that doesn't want us to know.

President Eisenhower made a trip to Palm Springs for a "winter holiday" between February 17 and 24 in 1954. On the evening of Saturday, February 20, he disappeared. When members of the press learned that the president was not where he should be, rumors ran rampant that he had either died or was seriously ill. There is circumstantial and testimonial evidence that President Eisenhower was at Murac Air Field (later named Edwards Air Force Base).

There are a number of sources alleging a meeting between Eisenhower and star beings that constituted a formal "First Contact Event." These sources are based on testimonies of military intelligence officers who witnessed the event, who read classified documents, saw films, or learned from their "insider contacts" of such a meeting. These testimonies describe what appear to have been two separate sets of meetings involving different star being groups who met either with the president and/or with Eisenhower administration officials over a short period of time. Reportedly, the first of these meetings did not lead to an agreement, and the star beings were rejected. (It is said they offered advanced space-travel technology under conditions that the Americans disband their nuclear capabilities. Eisenhower refused.)

A second meeting did culminate in an agreement, which has apparently been the basis of subsequent secret interactions with E.T. races involved in the treaty that was signed. There is some discrepancy in the sequence of meetings and where they were held, but all who have spoken out agree that a "First Contact" meeting involving President Eisenhower did occur and that the first of these meetings occurred during his February 1954 visit to Edwards Air Force Base.

Testimony supporting a First Contact with Eisenhower came from Charles L. Suggs, a retired sergeant from the U.S. Marine Corps. His father, Charles L. Suggs (1909–1987) was a former commander with the U.S. Navy who attended the meeting at Edwards Air Force Base with Eisenhower. Sergeant Suggs recounted his father's experience:

"I accompanied President Ike along with others on February 20. We met and spoke with two white-haired 'Nordics' [a species of star being called Nordics because of their appearance]. They had pale blue eyes and colorless lips. The Nordic spokesmen stood a number of feet away from Ike and would not let him approach any closer. A second Nordic stood on the extended ramp of a biconvex saucer that stood on a tripod landing gear on the landing strip. There were B-58 Hustlers on the field, even though the first one did not fly officially until 1956. These visitors said they came from another solar system. They posed detailed questions about our nuclear testing."

I should point out that this meeting occurred ten days before the Bravo testing of a fifteen-megaton hydrogen bomb on the

Bikini Atoll. The destructive force of the Bravo bomb was a thousand times more powerful than the atomic bombs at Nagasaki and Hiroshima. Perhaps the star beings called the meeting, alarmed at the possible consequences of the U.S. testing program.

Another testimony came from a former U.S. Air Force test pilot and colonel. He desired to remain anonymous because of his secrecy oath, but he gave the following details to a member of the British aristocracy, Lord Clancarty: "The pilot says he was one of six people at the meeting. Five alien craft landed at the base. Two were cigar-shaped and three were saucer-shaped. The aliens looked humanlike, but not exactly. The aliens spoke English, and supposedly informed the president that they wanted to start an 'educational program' for the people of Earth."

It was becoming obvious that there were several (or more) star beings present on the Earth. There was a consensus of this opinion, which included Master Sergeant Robert Dean, who had access to top secret documents while working in the intelligence division for the Supreme Commander of a major U.S. military command. In Dean's military career, he served at the Supreme Headquarters, Allied Powers Europe, where he witnessed the following documents while serving under the Supreme Allied Commander of Europe.

"There was a group (of aliens) that looked exactly like we do. There were two other groups. There was a very large group who were six to eight, sometimes nine feet tall, and they were humanoid but very pale, very white, and didn't have any hair on their bodies at all. There was another group that had sort of a reptilian quality to them. They had vertical pupils in their eyes, and their skin seemed to have the quality of what you would find on the stomach of a lizard. Military people and police officers all over the world have run into these. The 'Greys' were the fourth group: small; wiry; slanted, wraparound eyes; and no obvious procreative organs."

A man named Gerald Light, who was a gifted clairvoyant, a highly educated writer and lecturer, was part of a delegation that was invited to witness the presence of E.T. beings in order to study their reactions vis-à-vis panic, etc. Others in the delegation were Edwin Nourse of Brookings Institute (Truman's financial adviser) and Bishop MacIntyre of Los Angeles.

Light said that it was his understanding that Eisenhower would ignore the terrific conflict between the various "authorities" about revealing the contact with star beings and go directly to the people via radio and television. He expected an official statement testifying to the presence of star beings about the middle of May of 1954. The official announcement never came. Light describes the panic and confusion of many of those present at the official encounter as the reason for continuing the secrecy. He says the emotional impact and the differences of opinion as to what to divulge to the public and how each responded to extraterrestrial visitors were so life-changing that no one could agree on how to share what they had experienced or *whether* to reveal it.

Later in 1954, it was reported that another race of aliens who had been orbiting the Earth landed at Holloman Air Force Base in New Mexico. (New Mexico seems to be a favorite place for contacts.) The race identified themselves as originating from a planet around a red star in the constellation of Orion, known as Betelgeuse. They stated that their planet was dying and that in the future they would not be able to survive there. There have apparently been many meetings at Holloman Air Force Base.

Apparently, there was a treaty that was finally reached with "the Greys." It was called the Greada Treaty and states that the Greys would not interfere in our affairs and we would not interfere with theirs. We would keep their presence on Earth a secret. In exchange, they would furnish us with advanced technology, and we would allow them to abduct humans on a limited and periodic basis for the purpose of medical examinations and the monitoring of our human development, with the stipulation that the humans would not be harmed, would be returned to their point of abduction, would have no memory of the event (the Greys were proficient in mind control, which they subsequently shared with intelligence groups), and the Greys would furnish the government with a list of all human contacts and abductees on a regularly scheduled basis.

Dr. Michael Wolf served on various policy-making committees attached to the government for twenty-five years. He has membership in both the New York Academy of Sciences and the American Association for the Advancement of Science, and an MD from McGill Medical School in Montreal; a PhD from Cal Tech in computer science and theoretical physics; and a PhD from MIT in theoretical physics. He was chancellor of the New England Institute for Advanced Research, which started in 1982 as a think tank for the National Security Council. Dr. Wolf claims that the Eisenhower administration decided to circumvent the Constitution of the United States by entering into an agreement with an alien nation and that the treaty was never ratified as constitutionally required.

Don Phillips, a former Air Force serviceman and employee on clandestine aviation projects, testifies that he viewed a film and saw documents describing the meeting between President Eisenhower and extraterrestrials. He says we have records from 1954 that there were meetings between our own leaders in America and E.T.s that took place in Palm Springs. He says we were asked by the E.T.s if we would allow them to be here and do research. Our reply (on film) was, "How can we stop you? You are so advanced." It was Eisenhower who made the decision at that meeting.

Colonel Philip Corso, Eisenhower's National Security Advisor (who had done the research on the Roswell crash), has stated publicly, "We negotiated a kind of surrender with them (E.T.s) as long as we couldn't fight them. They dictated the terms because they knew what we feared the most was disclosure [of their presence]." Corso claims that he was not happy with the "negotiated surrender" because he viewed them [E.T.s] as a national security threat.

General Douglas MacArthur gave a similar warning in October 1955, suggesting that E.T. presence threatened human sovereignty. He said, "You now face a new world, a world of change. We speak in strange terms, of harnessing the cosmic energy, of ultimate conflict between a united human race and the sinister forces of some other planetary galaxy. The nations of the world will have to unite, for the next war will be an interplanetary war. The nations of the Earth must someday make a common front against attack by people from other planets."

In fact, it soon became obvious that the aliens had broken the agreement. They were not submitting a complete list of human contacts and abductees, and not all abductees were being returned. They were also harming the abductees psychologically (hence the work of Dr. John Mack at Harvard University's Department of Psychiatry, which I'll discuss in the next chapter). The aliens altered the agreement until they finally decided they wouldn't abide by it at all. The agreement and treaty had been with the Greys. There were, however, many other space beings represented on Earth who were more honorable.

According to Michael Wolf, there were several species of Greys. There were the short Greys from the fourth planet of the star system Zeta Reticulum. There were the tall Greys from Betelgeuse, the Orion star constellation. The tall Greys were said to be the overseers of the short Greys. Dr. Wolf says the Greys have positive intentions that have been hijacked by rogue elements of the U.S. military intelligence. The tall Greys were know to be the ambassadors of Orion and had agreements with U.S. Air Force generals. It was the job of the tall Greys to hold the short Greys in line.

The uncertainty over the motivations and behavior of the Grey star beings probably played a large role in the government's decision not to disclose the E.T. presence and the treaty that Eisenhower signed with them. The following passage from an official document leaked to me describes the official secrecy policy adapted in April 1954, right after Eisenhower's meeting in Palm Springs: "Any encounter with entities known to be of E.T. origin is to be considered to be a matter of national security and therefore classified TOP SECRET. Under no circumstances is the general public or the public press to learn of the existence of these entities. The official government policy is that such creatures do not exist and that no agency of the Federal Government is now engaged in any study of extra-terrestrials or their artifacts. Any deviation from this stated policy is absolutely forbidden."

There have been testimonies by former military intelligence officers who admit that their primary jobs were to hide, tamper with, or destroy evidence associated with star being presence. In my research I found that John Maynard, a military intelligence analyst for the Defense Intelligence Agency for twenty-one years, revealed the following in an interview in October 2001: "I became involved in [UFOs] while overseas in Germany, Turkey, and Korea. These areas were not noted for a lot of UFO activity. I was primarily afforded the opportunity to investigate peripherally a few incidents and implement disinformation or misinformation programs to divert attention away from the military and toward the paranormal and/or UFO [followers] in these areas. However, a point I never revealed to the military was that my grandmother brought me up believing that UFOs existed.

"Regardless of that point, I was still a staunch conservative politically, and placed my military duties ahead of my beliefs. I had a 'country, duty, and honor' type attitude. I believed that because of my dedication, and what appeared to be naïveté on my part, my military superiors did not question my actions when it came to debunking UFO sightings. However, I became very intrigued as to why UFOs were not to become public knowledge and that they (the government) preferred that any UFO information for public consumption stay in the realm of the paranormal and/or unreliable UFO resources.

"It took me several years to figure out that this blatant disregard for public opinion was a plan designed to keep and maintain the pressure of proof on certain elements of our society. The plan was basically to place the burden of proof on the UFO researchers and to steer the public away from the military organizations that were directly involved in UFO research. In this plan I deduced that the military was using the media to keep those UFO researchers from making too much of the issue by having the media brand them as kooks, weird, paranoid, and unbelievable; better yet, by having people who go around chasing after shadows in a belief that UFOs are real and the government is hiding something. To date, this plan has worked well above average, and the general public still has an opinion that follows whatever the media tells them."

Since the creation of controversy, intimidation, uncertainty, and confusion are the M.O. of military intelligence in order to ensure complete secrecy of the E.T. presence, it is, in my opinion, a testament to the courage of certain human beings when they do have the strength to reveal the most awe-inspiring (good and bad) truth since the beginning of man.

Another "conspiratorial" topic of conversation involves what is known as the Bilderberg Group. The original conference of this group was held at the Hotel de Bilderberg near Arnham from May 29 to May 31, 1954; hence the name. The Bilderberg Group included Nelson Rockefeller and other world financiers, Dean Rusk (later Secretary of State), Denis Healy (later British Minister of Defense), and other Western power leaders in the financial and political world. Their theme was "a means of Western collective management of the world order." One of the items for discussion was the possibility of extra-planetary life.

Some books allege a connection between the Bilderberg Group and the Council on Foreign Relations, but I have found no connection between the two in my own research. As one official told me, "It became an ongoing subject for discussion." He also said, "When the time comes, we will introduce extraterrestrials to the people of Earth and welcome them even though they have been here since the beginning of time and have been living in our place, date, space, and time. They are the diplomatic corps of the cosmos."

The American scientists received the largest share of high-level technology from the E.T.s: gene-splicing, cloning, aerospace ceramics, stealth technology, particle-beam devices, and gravity-control flight. Dr. Michael Wolf revealed in his book, *The Catchers of Heaven,* that he worked with E.T.s as part of his governmental duties. "I met with extra-terrestrial individuals every day in my work and shared living quarters with them." He said the Greys worked in underground facilities as requested by the U.S. government military intelligence. He also worked with Nordics from the Pleiadians star system.

Wolf also says that in 1954 the United States had four extra-terrestrial corpses in Hangar 18 at Wright-Patterson Air Force Base, Dayton, Ohio. He said those bodies came from a series of retrievals of downed UFOs. "The first UFO came down in 1941," he said. "It came down in the ocean west of San Diego and was retrieved by the Navy." (Naval intelligence has held a leadership position in UFO matters ever since.) Wolf also says there was another crash in 1946 as well as two other crashes in 1947.

My research revealed there were several crashes in 1934: one in Cumberland Gap, West Virginia, in February 1934; another off the coast of Boston, March '34; another explosion and crash in a swampy area of North Carolina in April '34; and another in Bristol, Virginia, November '34. Of course I find it synergistic that so many E.T. crashes happened during the year I was born, and in Virginia, where I was born.

I think about what we were told Vietnam was all about (however confusing that was!), and what else seemed to be going on from my perspective. In the research I have done since the war and also in talking to people who were willing to speak honestly, Vietnam was another story of cover-ups and disinformation. General George S. Brown, Air Force Chief of Staff, said at a press conference, "I don't know if this story has ever been told, but UFOs plagued us in Vietnam during the war."

In June of 1966 at Nha Trang, an active base on the coast-line of South Vietnam, a UFO approached, descended in full view of numerous soldiers, hovered a few hundred feet off the ground, and illuminated the entire area. The base generator failed and the base was blacked out. Idling aircraft engines, bulldozers, trucks, and diesel engines all failed for about four minutes. Then the UFO went straight up and rapidly disappeared from view.

Colonel Robert M. Tirman, an Air Force flight surgeon, was among those who observed what he called a huge cylindrical UFO on March 14, 1969, in Southeast Asia. Tirman was a passenger on a KC-135 with pilots and crew who also reported they saw the object. "The craft hovered in a vertical orientation about two miles from our plane at about fifteen-thousand feet altitude," he said. "When we tried to circle for a closer look, the UFO disappeared. Jet interceptors were scrambled and could not locate the UFO."

There were times when the occupants of whole villages disappeared after reports that UFO crafts were above their huts.

As more and more government documents become unclassi-fied, and retired high-ranking officials release their experiences, we will find more and more covert operations uncovered. A retired OSS/CIA man who was involved with the government military side of UFO investigations told me: "Executive branch knowl-edge of extraterrestrial data was placed under the watch of the OSS with the creation of this military/private sector government agency in 1942. It was deemed that the executive branch of the government had no 'need to know' as the power of the country does not reside there."

Another retired CIA spook who was in Vietnam told me, "The reason there is no information on Vietnam and E.T.s is that Colby [CIA director and former OSS] was in charge of covert and black ops in Vietnam. No one will have the whole story—ever. It's not just buried, it's been cremated."

I have discussed the UFO phenomenon with President Jimmy Carter. He told me he tried to shed some sunshine laws on military intelligence when he was president because he had actually seen a craft and wanted to know more (he wrote about his encounter when he was governor of Georgia). But he said elected officials are told such things only on a "need-to-know" basis. President Clinton was curious, too, but when he insisted on knowing more, he ran into a blank wall. The military intelligence extraterrestrial complex is, in effect, its own permanent government.

Reagan had seen a craft when he was still an actor, as he and Nancy were driving on Mulholland Drive in Los Angeles. Apparently the craft landed and an occupant descended, who then spoke to him telepathically. He never told me this directly, but he did tell a party of people who were waiting for him at Helen and Armand Deutch's house. Lucille Ball told me he had arrived ashen and confused, and told her the story. She told me because, as a Democrat, she wanted people to know that Ronnie must have been crazy . . . she didn't understand who she was talking to! I knew Ronnie visited the psychic Peter Hurkos frequently, and we all know about Nancy's astrologer. Reagan actually brought up possible ET invasions during his debates with Walter Mondale. I always wondered why the press didn't follow up on such a point of view—they chalked it up to "California Bizarre" I guess.

When I was in the Soviet Union and Washington, D.C., I became friendly with Roald Sagdeev, who was the head of the Soviet space program. He told me UFOs were real and came from the stars, but he wouldn't discuss it further. I thought it interesting that he married President Eisenhower's granddaughter.

Paul Hellyer, the ex-secretary of defense of Canada, is a friend of mine and is now publicly protesting the weaponization of space because he feels that we are being visited by "friendly" star beings who decry the military buildup on behalf of all the star nations. Paul and I have often discussed a government operation that has its roots in the final days of World War II and is still in effect to this day: Operation Paperclip. In the spring of 1945, many top German rocket scientists were welcomed to this country by military intelligence in order to work for America and to ensure their knowledge and abilities didn't fall into the hands of the Soviets. Over time, the mission of Operation Paperclip evolved into what it is today: to continually reinforce the military-industrial complex. In order for this to happen, there needed to be a constant fear of some kind. The areas of fear they agreed upon, to be called on at any time, were Communists, terrorists, asteroids, and extraterrestrials. Fear of all these things has been used to justify the weaponization of space.

Paul himself has never had an encounter or a sighting, but he knows of the experiences that happened to Carter and Reagan, and is aware of the meeting Eisenhower is supposed to have had in Palm Springs. He is aware of Area 51 and other military "secret" locations where the study of star beings and their advanced technology occurs. He sees that the fear and ridicule of celestial presence is motivated by the necessity to continue to build the military-industrial complex.

We've met and discussed those issues several times because he is most concerned about the financing of weapons in space where the celestials are far more advanced than we are anyway. He has discussed these things with Rep. Dennis Kucinich of Ohio, who had a close sighting over my home in Graham, Washington, when I lived there. Dennis found his encounter extremely moving. The smell of roses drew him out to my balcony where, when he looked up, he saw a gigantic triangular craft, silent, and observing him. It hovered, soundless, for ten minutes or so, and sped away with a speed he couldn't comprehend. He said he felt a connection in his heart and heard directions in his mind. He said military helicopters were out searching the area for the next few days. So others in the area must have seen it, too.

Paul Hellyer and I shared our knowledge of other people's experiences, which I would like to share now with you, dear Reader.

# chapter

8

BECAUSE I HAVE ALWAYS LOVED TO TRAVEL, I HAVE BEEN
privileged to construct a worldview that is maybe a little more
extensive than most people's, and now I am amending my worldview to a cosmic view. I think that's more accurate. Unidentified
flying crafts have been seen all over the world by every kind of
person imaginable. But probably the most prevalent these days
are the sightings over Mexico. My friend Lee Elders, a prominent
UFO investigator, has documented hundreds of sightings and
has a video library of thousands. Neither he nor many prominent
Mexicans can understand why such events, which are reported
on the front pages of the Mexican papers and are prominent
stories on respected news programs, are not even mentioned in
the American papers. Bill O'Reilly on Fox News did run a story
on the Mexican phenomena, but he basically ridiculed it. Lee
thinks the Mexican people in the largest city in the world are
open to the visitors because in their Catholic religion, they accept
miracles, and the sightings are considered miracles.

I asked my friend Mike Wallace and some others why there is such a blackout. He didn't have an answer, but then he doesn't believe they exist anyway. There has been no education in the journalistic world as to this reality, so they ignore it.

I have visited Mexico with Lee Elders and his wife, Brit, several times. We took a famous Mexican journalist, Jaime Maussan, with us on a number of star visitor stakeouts. Between them they had over five thousand videos of UFOs in the skies.

The mass sightings in Mexico are unparalleled in UFO research history. Fleets of them are spotted over every city, particularly Guadalajara, Leon, and Mexico City. They seem to come on special occasions so they will be observed by more people. On January 1, 1993, New Year's Day, there were five hours of continual UFOs above. In 1994, the first appearances of what were called fleets of them appeared. On January 29, 1994, there were five near misses reported by airplane pilots who complained to air traffic control, but nothing was done. During July 11, 1991, a total solar eclipse occurred, accompanied by UFOs who heralded it.

When the Pope visited Mexico City on January 25–26, 1999, there were two days of sightings which the people felt were welcoming their *Papa*. Each Mexican Independence Day celebration of September 16, 1991, 1992, and 1993 was accompanied by UFOs flying under their airplanes! They seemed to be crying out for public acknowledgment.

None of these events was printed or reported in the United States. There were videos of people filming from the tops of cars, out of windows, on city streets—everywhere. One journalist called Lee for contacts relating to a UFO story. Lee said he'd set him up with some authentic sources as long as the story was told seriously. He never heard back from the journalist.

In the old days during the Cold War, we could understand the blackout from a security point of view, but why does it still persist? Could it really be that people are afraid of risking their reputations, jobs, or scientific credibility just by asking for more information?

I met with President Menon when I was in Argentina. He not only understood that star visitors were present, he encouraged his military to contact them if possible.

The question that always comes up with people who study the purpose of celestial travelers is a karmic one. Do they, with their superior technological abilities, have the right to interfere with our free will destiny here on Earth? I have asked myself that often. I'm told that people they have actually contacted report that the star beings' deepest concern is for our environment. They say we are dangerously close to polluting the Earth beyond repair, which would, of course, include the human race.

Yet the star beings say that without our acknowledging their presence, they are karmically bound not to help us unless we ask for help. They long to give it to us, but will refrain as they respect our free will to kill ourselves. I have been told that on some levels they are allowed to interfere if we go nuclear, because such a disaster would affect them, the cosmos, and their own worlds. But biochemical warfare is up to us and is our problem.

One of the star beings cases that I find most credible and fascinating is the Billy Meier case in Switzerland. Lee and Brit Elders investigated that case for years and wrote an incredible coffee-table book called *UFO: Contact from the Pleiades*. I visited Billy with the Elders in his village, Hinderschmudruti, in Switzerland in 1981. For about two weeks I listened to his stories about contact with the Pleiades.

Billy Meier had UFO contact when he was a child. He was a lonely and isolated child, beaten by his father and ignored by his mother, when he was first contacted out in a field. The craft landed, and an older man descended, who gave him encouragement and love. Billy told me later that for a personal contact to occur, the human needed to shut down his mind and close off from the third-dimensional reality. In such despair he, as a child, had done just that—shut down from life. He had blocked it out, withdrawn, and by doing so had changed the frequencies of his mind. He later learned to do such a thing with his mind, and the crafts continued to come and teach him.

Now as an adult, about twice a month at about 2 A.M. he would go out into the countryside for a craft contact. We didn't follow because he told us that the Pleiadians did mental frequency scans on whoever might be following him, and if they found that indeed, he was being followed, they wouldn't be there when he arrived. We didn't want to be responsible for terminating a contact. Billy asked us not to follow him, and we respected that.

We would be up and waiting for him at dawn to hear about his experiences. He wrote them down, which have come to be called "The Contact Notes." I have read them all.

Billy had contacts and conversations with a Pleiadian woman called Semjase. She was quite beautiful, blond, had a nice body, and looked like a human. She told stories of how her forefathers were our forefathers. She said she and her celestial race felt duty-bound to the citizens of Earth. She said they were far from being perfect and are always evolving, just as we are. She said they were neither superior, superhuman, nor missionaries. She said humans would regard them as gods if they appeared to more than a few. Such a thing had happened in the past as recorded in the Bible:

"The Gods walked among us"; "The sons of Gods found the daughters of men fair." And they didn't want to risk it again.

Semjase said that her people had experienced the same severe problems and monumental decisions facing us, approximately thirty centuries ago. They have since evolved in knowledge, social structure, science, and technology with the help of more-advanced beings than themselves. Their purpose now is focused upon creating an awareness that other intelligent life exists in the universe, both good and bad by our standards, human and non-human in form.

She said that several times they have tried to establish terrestrial contact with humans but found them not to be sufficiently willing or loyal. Still others were afraid of other humans and the contact went unreported because they were sure they would be considered either liars or mad.

She said some intelligence organizations were busy studying their spacecraft, but did not always have available authentic photographs. Some were outright falsifications. She said they have learned all Earth languages and have perfected mental telepathy. She said they do not reach for an end to the universe because it doesn't exist, and that a single second in the "timeless" amounts to many millions of years in normal space. That was the reason why highly evolved spiritual beings could live for hundreds of years.

The Pleiadians call us their younger brothers and say that if we cannot solve our problems brought on by the imbalance of our technological advances and our ideological and religious differences, we will likely not be as fortunate as they, because we presently have no escape routes and are not prepared for this dilemma. They said man cannot reach the outer expanses of space until he achieves a hyperspace velocity. Then nonspace and nontime are reduced to almost nothing. Only then can man accomplish the light-years of our calculations.

She said many space travelers have visited our planet on many occasions (108 different civilizations at last count), coming from very distant systems. Encounters with the general public are not in their best interests at this time. They select individuals and monitor their thought frequencies and physical reactions over many years until one has been accepted, based on their standards and criteria. Then they draw them telepathically into remote locations for direct contact.

She said they don't measure time by our standards. They measure time by events. Human events on our Earth help them measure our evolutionary pattern and alert them to our progress. She said major events and the critical nature of these events are preprogrammed and can be altered only by a mass change of consciousness and awareness. But mankind does control its own destiny by the free will of effecting a mass consciousness change, which they would love to see. However, the Pleiadians and other "Beings of Light" do not see humanity taking control of our destiny in a positive way. They fear that we are rushing headlong to our own destruction and are bent on destroying all forms of life on this planet as well as critical life-support systems. At this stage in our evolution, they and other star beings are deeply saddened by this, as they consider us their younger brothers, separated only by a different time and a different space.

They travel at speeds many times the speed of light and can make it from their Pleiadian star system to Earth in seven hours, with the help of sublight speeds for atmospheric travel and hyperspace drive systems for travel at many times the speed of light.

They said our scientists were working on a "tachyon" system whose principles are the same.

She said that God is *of* creation, and we can't separate God from the creation because God itself is part of it, with all the rest of the "gods" who coexist with it in various states of being. She said that by creative thinking man acquires knowledge and wisdom and a sense of unlimited strength, which unbinds him from the limitations of convention and dogma. When the universal spirit manifests itself in the human being, then and only then can we reach the destination of our existence. She went on to say that they do not come on behalf of a god to bring to the world the long-awaited peace. They do not come on behalf of anyone, including themselves, since creation confers no obligation on them. Creation is a law unto itself, and every form of life must conform with it and become a part of it. They are spiritual beings who want to help us see what creation's conformity is. She said they had no authority to interfere by force with terrestrial concerns.

For the present, she said the Earth human holds the weight of his destiny on his own shoulders. However, should a time arise when they would find it necessary to involve themselves in certain matters pertaining to Earth, it would be done to prevent an aberration or possible cataclysm that would affect the depths of cosmic space beyond the conscious thoughts of the Earth human.

She said that thought transmission was the purest form of communication since the conversation could not be manipulated into something it is not. She said a human could deliver himself from all ignorance if he or she generated the will to seek the truth. She said enemies and attackers contribute to the growth of a spiritually developing person, so we must not see enemies as enemies: They are teachers. She said evolution is achieved only through spiritual development and the understanding that we are all one.

She said that when a being is happy, luck appears everywhere in his or her life because luck is a self-created state and comes from within the individual. It is a quality of the inner being and an inseparable spark of the spirit, which contains infinite force in its existence. She said Love is the instrument with which one may spread the eternal force that can never be extinguished, which overcomes death, and spreads light, which embodies the poise of wisdom, peace, and all that exceeds understanding.

She said wisdom is the mark of a human who has recognized the existence of his spirit and works with it according to the creational laws. One cannot clothe love in words, because love is the same as bliss, a state without a place. It is imperishable and cannot be shaped or manipulated into what it is not.

She said a wonder is merely the spiritual force exercising perfection, but all too often the human conceals a wonder behind a veil of mystery because he lacks any possible logical explanation. Something that has not been previously experienced is always considered a great mystery.

She said if we genuinely pooled all of our intelligence and imagination toward peace, we could achieve their level of evolvement in a few hundred years.

My time with Billy was mind-bending. I never saw the crafts, but many of the villagers in Hinderschmudruti did. Children and adults alike. Later, Billy told me what happened to his life: Friends swarmed around him until soon they felt they should take over. Some stole the pictures he had taken and others were paid off to betray him. He had at least seven assassination attempts on his life (he suspects disgruntled religious fanatics). He saved some metal samples from one of the crafts and gave them to Lee and Brit Elders.

Then the disinformation campaign started, which is usually the case. Disinformation surfaced from sources and quarters Billy couldn't define. Billy began to feel he was crazy (usually the case), and he withdrew from his "friends." He had been subjected to hours and hours of fourth-dimensional teachings on board a craft while living in his third-dimensional body. The confusion became too much for him. The frequencies collided, so to speak. Later, he went into complete withdrawal and wouldn't communicate with Lee or Brit or me. He didn't go out on his moped anymore either. He wanted nothing to do with any of it anymore.

In the meantime, Lee and Brit took the metal samples to several laboratories, said they thought they were authentic metal samples from a spacecraft, and were turned down flat. Finally, a senior scientist from IBM, Marcel Vogel, accepted them to have a look, and he was properly astonished. He said the metal was bonded by a crystal cold fusion technique we humans don't know how to do. He gave them a long and complicated technical description. He finally said that he just didn't know what to do with them. The samples he had were later stolen.

The struggle for the Elderses to find further scientific authentication was formidable. "Everyone was afraid even to look," they told me. "Afraid of their reputations, their credibility, and their standing in the scientific community."

The Elderses had corroboration from many witnesses. They had day- and nighttime photographs, the metal samples, sound samples, and, of course, the information Billy shared with them.

But Billy was cutting people out of his life. He couldn't take the pressure or the betrayals. Finally, he and his wife divorced. Fox TV heard about the divorce and did a TV special on UFOs produced by Bob Kiviat, which attacked Billy's credibility with the help of his wife.

Billy's case experience and all the Elderses' work on it went on the shelf. It was all very disappointing and a comment on what extraterrestrial material had in store for itself where human receptivity is concerned. I feel it is probably the most authentically researched case in modern UFO history.

In the meantime, I started researching what credible people had gone public to say, if for no other reason than I wanted to set the record straight for my grandchildren. I liked being an eccentric senior citizen who searched out new (old!) truth with the time I had left. And I wasn't going to quit until I quit. Let me share with you some of my research.

When the long-awaited solution to the UFO problem comes, I believe that it will prove to be not merely the next small step in the march of science, but a mighty and totally unexpected quantum leap.

> —*Dr. J. Allen Hynek, scientific consultant for*
> **Air Force Project Blue Book, the UFO Experience:**
> **A Scientific Inquiry,** *1972*

I can assure you that flying saucers, given that they exist, are not constructed by any power on Earth.

> —*President Harry S. Truman, April 4, 1950,*
> **White House conference**

Because of the developments of science, all countries of Earth will have to unite to survive and make a common front against attack by people from other planets. The politics of the future will be cosmic and interplanetary.

> —*General Douglas MacArthur, October 1955,*
> The New York Times

We have indeed been contacted—perhaps even visited—by extraterrestrial beings, and the U.S. government, in collusion with the other national powers of the Earth, is determined to keep this information from the general public.

> —*Victor Marchetti, former special assistant to the*
> *executive director for the CIA, in an article written*
> *by him for* Second Look *entitled "How the CIA*
> *Views the UFO Phenomenon"*
> *Washington, D.C., May 1979*

I strongly recommend that there be a committee investigation of the UFO phenomena. I think I owe it to the people to establish credibility regarding UFO's and to produce the greatest enlightenment on the subject.

> —*President Gerald Ford, in a letter he sent as a*
> *Congressman to the chairman of the Armed Services*
> *Committee*
> *March 28, 1966*

Unknown subjects are operating under intelligent control . . . It is imperative that we learn where UFO's come from and what their purpose is.

> —*Admiral Roscoe Hillenkoetter, first director of the*
> *CIA, 1947–50*

More than 10,000 sightings have been reported, the majority of which cannot be accounted for by any scientific explanation . . . I am convinced that these objects do exist and that they are not manufactured by any nation on Earth. I can therefore see no alternative to accepting the theory that they come from some extraterrestrial source.

> —*Air Chief Marshal Lord Dowling, commander-in-chief of the Royal Air Force Fighter Command during the Battle of Britain, printed in the* **Sunday Dispatch**
> **London, July 11, 1954**

I don't laugh at people anymore when they say they've seen UFOs. I've seen one myself.

> —*President Jimmy Carter, remarking on his sighting in January 1969*
> **ABC News, January 1999**

The phenomenon reported is something real and not visionary or fictitious.

> —*General Nathan Twining, chairman, Joint Chiefs of Staff, 1955–58*
> *September 23, 1947*

The number of thoughtful, intelligent, educated people in full possession of their faculties, who have 'seen something' and described it grows every day. . . . We can say categorically that mysterious objects have indeed appeared and continue to appear in the sky that surrounds us.

> —*General Lionel M. Chasin, commanding general of the French Air Forces, and the general air defense coordinator of the Allied Air Forces of NATO*

If the intelligence of these UFO's creatures were sufficiently superior to ours, they might choose to have little, if any, contact with us.

> —*Brookings Institute (in a report on extraterrestrial life)*, **New York Times** *December 15, 1960*

Mankind are here because they are the offspring of parents who were first brought here from another planet. And power was given them to propagate their species. And they were commanded to multiply and replenish the Earth.

> —*Brigham Young*

Something unknown to our understanding is visiting the Earth.

> —*Dr. Mitrovan Zverov, Soviet scientist*

These objects (UFOs) are conceived and directed by intelligent beings of a very high order. They probably do not originate in our solar system, perhaps not even in our galaxy.

> —*Dr. Hermann Oberth, renowned rocket and space travel authority, and often called the Father of the V-1 and V-2 weaponry of World War II press conference in Innsbruck, Austria, June 1954*

In the distant future, we will encounter some other intelligent life.

> —*Frank Borman, astronaut*

As the next step in my research and investigation, I called my friend, Dr. John Mack of the Department of Psychiatry at Harvard, and asked him to fill me in on the research he had been doing on "experiencers," people who had been taken aboard crafts and needed psychiatric counseling as a result. Apparently over 3.5 million Americans have had that kind of "contact" with the star visitors. The numbers are much higher worldwide. John listened to many people who had come to him and finally decided that these were experiences which, to the "experiencers," were real.

Mack found that his venture into UFO abduction cases caused real controversy. Critics claimed that his work was an example of a kind of cult of irrationality and an exercise in antiscience and unreason. But he had a growing conviction in the authenticity of the "experiencers."

I remember reading a review by James Gleick in the *New Republic* that called Mack's work "an alien abduction mythology," a "leading case of the contrarational, antiscience cults that are flourishing with dismaying vigor in the United States." He lumped everything Mack was doing with "paranormals who bend spoons, parapsychologists who sense spiritual auras, crystal healers, believers in reincarnation, and psychic crime solvers, as well as tarot readers and crystal ball gazers." I wondered what that review did to John Mack's feelings and his standing at Harvard.

Mack told me, "The information I obtained during the years of this investigation has been communicated in case after case with such power and consistency that a body of data formed which seems to point clearly to the experiential truth of the contact phenomenon, whatever its ultimate source might prove to be." He went on to say that what the experiencers were describing cannot be explained according to our traditional scientific view. So it would seem to be more sensible and, indeed, more rational to change our scientific perspective and expand our notions of reality. He said the contact abduction phenomenon forces us to take it seriously and reexamine our perception of ourselves and human identity. In other words, to look at ourselves from a cosmic perspective.

Mack had the view that contact or abductions by star beings isn't so much about the events as it is about how we need to expand our sense of ourselves and, more importantly, our understanding of reality. He felt we should awaken our restricted potential as human explorers in this universe and see that it is rich in meaning and intelligence.

As I questioned him, he said none of those who had been taken aboard crafts seemed psychologically disturbed except in the secondary sense caused by the experience itself. He said there was little to suggest that their stories were delusional, fantasy, or dreams. He said the intensity of energy and emotions as the people relived their experiences was unlike anything he had encountered in his other clinical work. And the immediacy of his own presence, his support, and the understanding required had influenced the way he regarded the psychotherapeutic treatment in general. He said he had come to see that experiences aboard spacecraft had important philosophical, spiritual, and social implications and his work had led him to challenge the prevailing worldview of consensus reality which he had grown up believing and had always applied to his clinical and scientific endeavors.

He went on to say that there are other phenomena that have led to the challenging of the prevailing materialistic-dualistic worldview of reality. These include near-death experiences, meditation practices, the use of psychedelic substances, shamanic journeys, ecstatic dancing, religious rituals, out-of-body experiences, and any other practice that may open us to what we in the West call nonordinary states of consciousness. We know the physical world best. We do not have a real acquaintance with the world of consciousness in and around ourselves. The power of the consciousness, of course, is immense, and John Mack felt it was time for further exploration.

Most of the abductees and contactees that Mack treated were usually more open and intuitive individuals in their own lives than other "normal" people. They were less tolerant of societal authoritarianism and more flexible in accepting diversity and the unusual experiences of other people. I found John's definition of the Western scientific paradigm most important. "We have a rigid theology," he said, "and that belief system is held in place by the structures, categories, and polarities of language such as real/unreal, exists/doesn't exist, objective/subjective, intrapsychic/external world, and happened/did not happen." He said he tried to put aside all the language forms and simply collect raw experiential information, dispensing with any already-conceived-of worldview he might have. He said he regarded his "experiencers" as coinvestigators, and most of them found it quite easy to go into "nonordinary" states of consciousness.

The "aliens" or star beings often told them they should not remember what had occurred, either for their own protection or the protection of their families. Sometimes the experiencers felt they were disobeying the star people, whom they felt connected to on a very deep level, when they cooperated with Mack. Mack reassured them that no harm had ever come to anyone when the work was done in an appropriately supportive context.

I don't know the difference between what Billy Meier experienced and what John Mack's patients experienced, except for one thing. Billy always drove toward the craft and was then taken up. He wasn't abducted, seemingly against his will, though many of the experiencers went willingly, too. Many of them remembered encounters since childhood; some star beings were playmates or "little people," healers and teachers. However, when these children reached puberty, a fear set in, particularly when their parents told them they were only dreaming, and the beings weren't real. Mack said abductees and contactee experiencers run in families, sometimes over three generations or more.

The abductees complain of the switching off of memory and consciousness, and of a feeling of being floated through walls, doorways, and windows. Many of them have a feeling of inexplicable love as though they had gone home. They also experience great cycles of birth and death and relive powerful past life experiences.

The crafts vary in size. They are described as silvery or metallic, cigar-shaped, saucer-shaped, dome-shaped with colorful lights emanating from the bottom through portholelike openings. Then they are "floated" or "beamed" into the craft. Once inside, the abductee witnesses "alien" beings who are busy doing various tasks. The beings are described as all sorts. I remembered that Semjase had said over 108 different star being species are visiting Earth. Mack's research with his experiencers bears that out. The aliens seem fascinated with the humans, staring at them extensively, close to the human's head, with large eyes. The abductees feel that their minds are being read, even taken over.

I believe from most of Mack's experiencer descriptions that the predominant "abductors" are what is known as the "Greys." They are short (three to four feet high), and they move in a robotical way. There seems to be no gender difference. They are hairless with no ears and have rudimentary nostril holes and a thin slit for a mouth, which rarely opens or is expressive of emotion. The most prominent feature of this species are the huge black eyes that curve upward and are more rounded toward the center of the head and pointed at the outer edge. They seem to have no whites or pupils although sometimes one can see a life within the eye, as though the outer eye is a kind of goggle. The eyes seem to have a compelling power which the abductee, more often than not, wants to avoid, because of a feeling of loss of will and identity. There is a leader or a doctor who is in charge and toward whom the abductee feels a kinship bordering on love. Yet at the same time, the abductee resents the control the leader has over him. The communication between the two is done telepathically, with no common language necessary. They have large, pear-shaped heads that protrude in the back, long arms with three or four long fingers, thin torsos, and spindly legs. Feet are usually covered with single-piece boots. External genitalia are rarely observed. These beings have been portrayed in films such as *Close Encounters of the Third Kind,* and I wondered how the filmmakers conjured up the appearance.

As I've said, there seem to be many different species of "abductors." Some are tall and humanlike, some translucent, some solid. Some seem reptilian and carry out mechanical functions. Some are blond and Nordic-looking. But by far the most common "abductors" are the "Greys."

The experiences that Dr. John Mack told me about were nothing like what Billy Meier told me. But then his experience was with the Pleiadians, a different (and probably more advanced) species altogether. The procedures with the "Greys" vary slightly but they are generally probing and surgical-like. Skin and hair samples as well as samples from within the body are taken. Instruments are used to penetrate virtually every part of the body: nose, sinuses, eyes, ears, head, arms, legs, feet, abdomen, genitalia, and chest. Surgical procedures are done inside the head, which make the abductees feel as though their nervous systems have been altered. The most common procedures involve the reproductive system. They seem to be more interested in how we procreate than anything else. Sperm samples are taken from men and eggs are removed from women.

Abductees often report having been impregnated by the alien beings and later having the fetuses removed. I have had several women over the years call me with the trials of that experience. Some *knew* they were virgins, felt strange, had a sonogram that proved there was a fetus growing, and a few months later it disappeared. The same abductees later see a fetus (which they feel is theirs) in an incubator of some kind aboard the craft when they are abducted again. They feel they are seeing hybrids that belong to them. Experiencers say they see older hybrids, adolescents and adults, which the aliens tell them are their own, too.

John Mack feels that these Greys are incubating a hybrid race, either because they need more life on their planet or because they may be sensing the end of human life here on Earth. The "procedures" seem to have to do with some sort of genetic engineering for the purpose of creating human/alien hybrid offspring. All of the abductees talk about the information imparted to them concerning the fate of the Earth. They say humans are destructive and uncaring about nature. They show screens with images projected showing the ultimate fate of the Earth unless we change our ways. Scenes of Earth devastated by a nuclear holocaust, vast panoramas of lifeless, polluted landscapes and oceans, and apocalyptic images of giant earthquakes, firestorms, floods, and even fractures of the planet itself. These images are deeply disturbing to the abductees, who are sometimes given assignments to prevent such catastrophes.

When I was in Peru, I met several men who were taken aboard crafts and shown the same apocalyptic scenes on screens. One was shown a future scene that was to happen in his own village. It did happen, exactly as he was shown, some weeks later. Does this mean, I asked John Mack, that we have an already-determined future that can change only with a massive shift of consciousness? That makes the Bible Code, the prophecies, and the Bible (Revelation) a code that is really a PLAN. But who made the Plan? And was the Plan determined by the consciousness of the human race a long time ago? And by whom?

Abductees are often convinced that some sort of implant has been placed in their bodies so that they can be monitored. Many have consulted doctors who have indeed found foreign objects and removed them.

Mack said there were five consistent phenomena that occurred in all abductees:

1. High degrees of detailed consistency that was reported with emotion appropriate to the experience.

2. The absence of psychiatric illness or other apparent psychological or emotional factors that could account for what is being reported.

3. The physical changes and lesions affecting the bodies of the experiencers, which followed no evident psychodynamic pattern.

4. Independent observation of crafts by witnesses while the abductions were taking place.

5. The reports by children as young as two or three of having been abducted.

I met with Mack many times over a few years. He'd come to New Mexico or we'd arrange to meet in Los Angeles when we were both there. I admired his courage so much in the face of the ridicule he was tolerating from the academic community. But much to their credit, Harvard kept him on so that he could proceed with the pioneer work of studying perhaps the most important phenomenon on the planet—the "we are not alone" phenomenon.

He was kind and available to the abductees, who also sought solace with each other as they attempted to blend their experiences in with their lives. Many felt total isolation and estrangement from their families and friends. The children who were abducted were usually told they were either dreaming or lying, which motivated them to keep their mouths shut. Even adults were reluctant to talk except in the company of Mack or other abductees.

Not all of the abductees experienced invasive physical procedures, which led them and Mack to believe that certain of them were "selected" for either programming, seeding, enlightenment, spiritual leadership, or a deep study in the intricacies of human fear. Those spouses who were "selected" found it very difficult to carry on an intimate relationship with the spouse who wasn't selected. There was a decided resistance to accepting the reality of the experience by the spouse who didn't experience. Also, many marriages and relationships were disrupted because the experiencer's personal development was much more swift, leaving the other spouse behind.

Many abductees felt profound love for the alien beings, in some ways deeper than the love they felt for any human. Yet when their sperm or eggs were taken, they were conflicted by the intrusion, while at the same time feeling privileged to participate in the creation and evolution of new life. They spoke of a new understanding of universal love and connectedness. Mack thought it was possible that he was seeing relationship processes that were evolutionary in nature and not comprehensible in the linear terms of our familiar emotional constructs. For example, he said many of the abductees experience past lives with their alien friends, and that is the reason for the profound recognition and love. They felt that the cycles of birth and death gave them a different perspective about time and nature and the secrets of their own identity. The nature of their soul without a body became clear to them, enabling them to drop their ego and feel a sense of continuity with all life, and not just in this lifetime. Some of them felt they had gone home and experienced profound joy, and when they left the craft, often they wept with sadness because they were leaving their cosmic home. The alien identity seemed somehow to be connected to the soul and identity of the abductee. To me, this would explain who was "selected" and who wasn't.

One of the things each abductee reported was a feeling of the collapse of time and space, of being in multiple times and places simultaneously. This is what Einstein said: "All time is happening concurrently." The alien star beings told the abductees that they would remember what they needed to know. Most of them remembered more than they wanted to know. However, each abductee *knew* that the star beings were telling them the truth about what we were doing to our world with our politics, our food, the way we treat each other, and the pollution of our environment. They said the laws of the universe were different than ours on Earth and if we kept going as we were, the catastrophe would be inevitable. They said we have to spiritually rebalance ourselves before it is too late.

Mack admitted that in psychiatry it is very difficult to admit when we don't know or understand something. There is a tendency to fit psychological data or emotional phenomena into familiar categories. Total uncertainty is very uncomfortable. He said the star being alien abduction phenomenon was a rich source of information regarding how we understood ourselves and our surrounding universe. We had to admit that we really knew very little about nature, ourselves, and how we participated in the universe.

The abductees, regardless of the trauma of their experience, felt they were opened up to something, like they'd been given an intense jump into a spiritual realm they were not ready for. They wanted to become more spiritual even though they didn't know what that meant or how to do it. Some were shown pictures on a screen of their "real" alien family. Some said they'd always known they were different, that they weren't from here. They'd always wanted to run away—but to where?

Some said the aliens told them with great sadness that they had destroyed their own planet because of "something they had built." They were deciding whether they could live on this Earth with humans, but they found the humans too lonely, too incapable of sharing. In the alien world there were no secrets, everyone knew what everyone else was thinking. Humans were afraid of being hurt, not getting what they wanted, not opening up, and afraid of love. If we didn't change ourselves, nature would change us. Fear doesn't live as much in the consciousness of other worlds as it does here. And fear is difficult to live around. There is so much more freedom when there is less fear.

Mack was genuinely concerned for children that had been taken aboard crafts, whose parents then subjected them to doctors who gave them tests, destructive treatment, countless hours of medical examinations, wrong diagnoses, and inappropriate evaluations. He was saddened by the denial that most Earth families live in.

Many of his patients began to have dreams that covered a vast range of existential subjects: the nature of time, space, the cycles of birth, death, creation, the mystery of truth, spirit and soul, the limitations of material science. Some believed they were told to write about such things, and the information would be there for them. They were told that each of their souls was part of the whole, and they should give birth to their thoughts. One person received the information that "technical data does not lead to the discovery of other beings. Spiritual data does."

While some abductees felt love and compassion from the star beings, others felt they didn't care about them. They felt like specimens of interest and curiosity, but not with any compassion or heart. Most felt the star beings were superior and behaved that way, never asking if they could proceed with a procedure, just doing it. It was the feeling of helplessness that drove most of the abductees to terror. They felt they were not the masters of their own lives. However, after their experiences they began to feel an empathy for life itself on a more universal and global scale. They became troubled as to the fate of the Earth. Then they reevaluated their feelings of fear and loss of control because they felt the star beings were trying to do what they could to prevent the human suicide that was occurring on Earth. The genetic experiments and reproductive activity, then, were part of a bigger plan to help us humans.

The rage and anger that many of the abductees felt regarding the invasion of their privacy, the paralysis that was induced and the overall lack of respect for their will was exceedingly difficult for them to overcome. But little by little most seemed to agree that if *they* acted with rage and hostility, nothing could be accomplished. All said the problem was their own fear. They needed to learn a fear mantra. They all agreed the aliens were more advanced spiritually and emotionally and that they were trying to serve the future for humans as well as themselves.

As their attitudes changed, so did their own sensitivities. They began to feel other people's energy, their emotional states, their "auras," and, yes, their fears. They said if they processed the abduction properly, they felt themselves open up to a new world of sensitivity.

It sounded as though the star beings were putting many abductees through an examination of their deepest fears. Fear, they teach, is at the bottom of most human ills. But even if humans are saturated with it, they can get beyond it. Fear is the great barrier to enlightenment and understanding of oneself.

Many of the abductees expressed the fear of "facing themselves." The star beings used screens on which were projected scenes not only of events from the abductees' childhoods but also scenes from other lifetimes that the abductees *knew* were real. In this way they began to understand their "soul's journey" through time. I had heard of the screen teachings from many other people who had been taken aboard crafts, willingly or unwillingly. I began to wonder what "unwilling" really meant. Did it mean that a person was out of touch consciously with what he or she *unconsciously* had contracted to do? So many of us are not in touch with what we really want, need, or have, on a soul level, agreed to do. The abductees are served a lesson in time and space and experience that they are either ready for or desire to be ready for. Dr. John Mack was the observer and helpmate in those contracts. I asked him why *he* was the doctor who had agreed on such a deep level to hear and treat these experiences. What was his cosmic role in all of this? Why had he created this reality for himself, which could actually get him fired from the Department of Psychiatry at Harvard? He said he didn't really know except he always liked to help people who had experiences beyond the normal. John even arranged for some of his experiencers to speak to a psychiatry seminar group at the Cambridge Hospital in Boston. The largely skeptical psychiatrists and other mental health professionals were surprisingly open to the disarmingly sincere, yet astonishing stories the abductees told. The group of doctors was open to the "expansion of their own reality."

One of the abductees said "the alien beings were closer to the divine source than human beings seem to be, and it was possible that their presence among us, however cruel and traumatic, may be part of a larger process that was bringing us back to God, a journey that had taken many far from God and that many are tired of and are now working, flowing, and struggling to bring themselves back to their source."

Some of the abductees were more educated than others. The more educated an abductee was, the more complex was his assessment of what was occurring. "They are Earth gardeners," said one abductee of the aliens. "They are trying really hard to instruct us to find a plenitude and not to be caught in the human impulses toward extinction." If we explode this Earth paradise, it is a loss for the universe. The Earth is essential to the unity of the universe. We are in an apocalyptic final hour, and this must be met and challenged. We are experiencing a paradigm of initiation. We are being initiated while we initiate. When we accomplish our initiation, we will be less predatory and destructive. We need to gain a perspective as to where we belong in the universal order.

Many of the abductees were left with nightmares, severe stress syndromes, headaches, gastrointestinal symptoms, neuropathies, psychosexual dysfunctions, and, of course, fears. At the same time there was real evidence that the abductees had been healed of conditions ranging from pneumonia, leukemia, paralyzed limbs due to poliomyelitis. Many of them became healers themselves.

Though they continued to resent the abduction experiences, they also began to feel they were participating in a life-creating or life-changing process that had deep importance and value. All of them expressed a deepening commitment to the Earth and, if it took personal pain and terror to make them see that, it was worth it. They said birth of new points of view always included pain and fear. The "ego death" had enabled their spiritual growth and the expansion of their consciousness.

The experience of the "merging of time/space dimensions" brought on memories of long, long ago that they couldn't define, which caused them to question the Western concepts of scientific and philosophical ideology. They only knew now that human beings were not lords of the Earth, but children of the cosmos who needed to find their way to live in harmony with all kinds of species in the universe and on Earth. They said it was a humbling experience.

Many of them felt that they themselves had a dual human/ alien identity that gave them a soul link to the universal source of creation. And they became alarmed at the Western scientific, materialistic worldview that had resulted in creating weapons of destruction, tearing the Earth apart, and bringing the human species to the brink of extinction because we were so out of harmony with ourselves and nature. They began to become aware of the corporate business interests that controlled the monetary systems and believed that physical laws were the whole truth.

The UFO abduction phenomenon strikes at the very heart of the Western materialistic view of reality that requires that we be in control and be able to *prove* any theory. The scientific and governmental intellects that shape our view are confused and give us a garbled mixture of denial and cover-up that only fuels conspiracy theories. There is a naturalness beyond ourselves that is as true as what our consensus reality claims. Of course, the UFO abduction phenomenon presents astounding problems for religious leaders and the Church. It is one thing to believe in the physicalness of angels and to administer a belief in spirits to the flock of believers, but it is another to go along with angels and spirits who come in technologically advanced spaceships and teach that organized religion is one of mankind's serious problems. In such an instance, better to claim the star beings are playmates of the Devil. The Devil is always useful when a giant truth is incomprehensible.

As John Mack and I spoke together, we came to the conclusion (he as a skeptically convinced psychotherapist, and I as a believer) that human greed and control of nature were ravaging the Earth's ecosystems, bringing us to the edge of disaster, and the arrested development of human consciousness would render us *out of control* of that which we seemed to live our lives for. We needed help, and we needed to be open to it before it was too late. We also agreed that there seemed to be a concerted effort on the part of the star visitors to join two species (theirs and ours) for the creation of a new evolutionary life-form.

There was an almost mythical drama occurring on our plane of reality that was an evolution of a species joining, a repopulation of the Earth that would survive the environmental collapse we insisted on being blind to. A paradigm shift in consciousness would occur whether we realized it or not, only to announce the end of the exclusively empirical, rationalistic way of experiencing reality. We would then live in a universe different from the one we had been taught to believe in.

The United States leads in sheer numbers of UFO abductions, followed by England and Brazil, Argentina, Australia, Bolivia, Canada, Chile, Finland, France, Poland, South Africa, the Soviet Union, Spain, Uruguay, and West Germany (not necessarily in that order). China boasts the largest number of people who witnessed a single event . . . on April 24, 1981, one million Chinese witnessed a spiral-shaped UFO at the same time. There were no follow-up questions from the government or their media. Most of the UFO sightings are cloaked in secrecy or presented with disinformation.

I met and talked with John Mack for many years. He was a humble man and in many ways socially unsure of himself. I think he has done some of the most important work in our world to bridge the gap between consciousness and science. One of our last conversations had to do with his depression over the behavior of the George W. Bush administration. In fact, he was ready to give up his work at Harvard in order to work against Bush. I told him I thought we Americans deserved the experience of W.

so that we could resurrect the importance of democracy and our individual roles in it. I said I thought everything happens just as it should—whatever it was.

He sighed and said, "Let me think about that." He left for London a week later. A week after that, John Mack was killed by a hit-and-run driver on a street in London. His death was as mysterious as the material he was investigating. Bizarrely, another man named John Mack was killed by a drunk driver a few hours later in London on the same day.

I admired him as much as anyone I've ever known, and I will always miss him and his foresight and courage. I think I hear from him from time to time, and when I do, I listen carefully and feel inspired to keep asking questions.

When I was in South Africa playing in my one-woman show, I made contact with a man named Credo Mutwa. Credo is perhaps the most well-known *sangoma* or medicine man in and outside of South Africa. He has knowledge of the West and was raised as a Christian, but renounced it in order to become "the uplifter of his people." He is the spiritual leader of the *sanusis* and *sangomas* of South Africa. His knowledge of African spirituality and culture is unsurpassed. He has had relationships with the *mantindane*, which he describes as extraterrestrial givers of knowledge to humankind. He says the "grey aliens" taught him art, medicine, science, and engineering.

I visited him for two days in his village, Mafiking, northwest of Johannesburg. He is known as Vusumazulu, a name given to him during his initiation which means "awakening the Zulus." He was furious because he said "the people from the stars are trying to give us knowledge, but we are too stupid." I sat with him in his hut, surrounded by sculptures he had made of the star people. They seemed to represent many different species.

Credo was a huge and extremely nervous man. He wore colorful robes, and heavy metal adornments around his neck. There were bones, shells, ivory, and leather. He immediately spoke of the grey aliens as being parasitic beings who sowed discord. He told me about his abductions with aliens who he knew had been on Earth from the very beginning. "They belong here," he said. "They are our future descendants."

Credo had had a difficult and stressful life. He was raped as a young man and had been attacked by mobs during political crises. He was stabbed during the Soweto riots and was nearly burned alive by a mob. To be burned alive to an African means that your very soul is destroyed and cannot reincarnate again. This near-death experience changed his worldview. He said star people had been coming from the stars in sky boats since the beginning of time. He spoke of bright blue spheres, disk-shaped crafts, and the *mantindane* who took him and others to their magical vehicles. He said the extraterrestrials have covertly influenced and manipulated human cultures for all time from the shadows.

He said the men of his people have their semen drained by the *mantindane,* and the women are molested, but they also taught his people to drill through stone and how to protect themselves from smallpox. He said taller star people came from the sky and helped his people through famine by teaching the women how to grind and cook the poisonous cassava plant to make it edible to human beings.

He told me I would find many cultures reluctant to talk about the star people because they do things you can't imagine. "They walk through walls and do things that your mind cannot accept." But these are real beings, and they should be communicated with. "The skies are full of life," he said, "and the origin of life can be attributed to the stars."

"We revere the stars with fear and awe," he said. "All of our forefathers came from the stars. All of our lives have been changed by those who are not of this world." He described the star beings as varied. "Tall, blond beings, hairy creatures, entities with large heads, unnaturally pink skin, and a long male organ; creatures that wore helmets and armor to protect themselves from our world." He specifically called the Greys "sky monkeys." He said they put fetuses into his people's women and took them away later.

He said he has one star being who has been with him since he was a baby. "In the Catholic Church she would be called a 'demon,' but she was my guardian angel." He said she wore a skirt made of string and had reddish skin, heavy eyebrows, big wide-apart eyes, and spoke through a hole in her throat. "Sometimes she wears a fish-shaped helmet with a crest on it," he said. "And my aunt Nina is haunted and protected by her, too. This is no devil. Many *sangomas* and healers in Zululand are bothered and controlled by her because she can see the future."

After knowing me a few hours, Credo told me about the most significant of his abduction encounters. It was in 1958 while he walked in the sacred Inyangani Mountains in Rhodesia (now Zimbabwe). He was looking for herbs to treat his backache. He found the herbs and began to dig. He said he loved the smell of the earth, the trees, the animals, the air. Suddenly, he was aware of a strange silence. Then there was blue smoke. He could no longer see his surroundings. Next thing he remembered he was naked, encased in a tank. Then he was lying on a contoured table. He said he struggled to get off the table and urinated in the process, which embarrassed him. He said then he was completely paralyzed. He said he was surrounded by small "doll-like" beings about three feet tall with huge black eyes ("like nothing on Earth"). The noses of the creatures had small nostrils and the mouths were like a razor cut with no lips. They had no hair or ears, and four long thin fingers. They wore grayish silver shiny uniforms and a round cap. They walked about as though they were powered by batteries. There was a strange light that didn't seem electrical.

He said some kind of a big woman seemed to be in charge and stood close to him. She had no breasts, and others were afraid of her. The beings could walk right through the curtain that surrounded him. The big female put her hand over his mouth and patted it. He said none of the beings were really thinking about him. He was just a specimen. One of them stabbed something in his thigh, and something was stuck in his nose, which caused an explosion in his head. Credo said the fear and pain were reminiscent of his rape experience. He said he had learned to leave his body when he was frightened, but in this instance he couldn't.

Then he said a naked white woman came up to him. She touched his face and aroused him with her hand. Then she climbed on top of him "like a crazy Zulu girl." But he said this female being didn't seem real. She was cold, like she wasn't alive. "Then she attached something to my penis that caused me to ejaculate too much." As Credo told me the story, he smoked several cigarettes and became extremely emotional.

He remembered the pain and rocked back and forth. He said his penis was burning when the aliens pushed him off the table. Then one of them showed him something. It was a bottle filled with a pinkish liquid and inside was another creature he felt sure was an unborn human baby. "I will never forget this," he said.

Somehow he found himself back in the digging place, his trousers and shirt torn, and a dullness in his brain. He made his way to a village and realized he had been gone for three days. He said drops of blood were oozing from pores in his skin, and he itched. Then Credo showed me the scoop mark in his thigh which he attributed to the abduction. He said he felt close to madness, and it took him months to recover. Then he said the most horrifying memory was that the skin began to peel off his penis, which then developed sores. He says that that condition remained, which was why his first wife left him.

Other people in the village had had similar experiences but wouldn't talk to anyone about their "God-injuries" unless they had been through it. Later, after his stabbings in the Soweto riots, he was angry and depressed while recovering. He was visited by the Big Leader Woman. She moved toward him and brutally ripped off all his bandages and left. He said his wounds healed in one day.

As he told me his astonishing stories, he gathered some pictures he had painted and gave them to me. I still have them and will proudly hang them on the walls in my new house. I sometimes wonder if I'll be visited by the group through their portraits!

For all that he went through with the Greys (and others), he says they are "solvers of great problems." He urged me to tell all my American friends to stop arguing about whether they are real. "They are, and you should persuade your scientists to test these things instead of saying it's all nonsense." When I asked him why he thought there was such resistance in the West to acknowledge these star beings, he said, "The Western civilization believes that we human beings are the cocks of the walk in this world and that we humans are the highest evolved forms in the universe. We are not alone, and that is all there is to it."

He spoke also of what he called religious falsities, that there is only one God and no other. He said the cosmos has many great beings, and we should just announce that they are here. In spite of his negative assessment of their behavior toward him, he said he would gladly welcome their government over our human governments. "It would be the best thing that ever happened to the human race."

When I left Credo, I knew I would write about him someday. He would be part of a long list of memorable friends who had had similar experiences with star visitors. And as I write this, I realize I'm counting the countries I have visited where these astonishing reminders that we are not alone occurred. In nearly every country on the planet I have met people who thought I would take their experience with UFOs seriously. I have already mentioned Mexico in detail. But there are people in Sweden, Thailand, Germany, England, France, Italy, Russia, Tunisia, Japan, Korea, India, Australia, Brazil, Argentina, Cambodia, Egypt, Morocco, Tanzania, Kenya, Peru, Canada, China, and the United States.

I have thought a great deal about whether we citizens should enact a Truth Squad Request for more information from our intelligence services on the known presence of star beings on and around our planet. Steve Bassett is a registered UFO lobbyist who campaigns against the Truth Embargo on the part of our government. Neither he nor I understand why the Chinese, the Russians, and the Mexicans are more flexible on this truth than we are.

The star beings are apparently driving their disclosure on Earth so that they can be "helpful" to us regardless of the definition of their contribution. The star beings desire the ultimate form of social justice, which is to dispense the truth to Earth humans. Without knowledge of the truth of all the players, agreements cannot be reached. To move forward as a race and species in the universe, we must be told the truth.

Apocalyptic thinking is a tool of control if we are made to be fearful from lack of knowledge. If the fear of "extraterrestrials" is allowed to prevail, and the authentic presence of ETs is denied in the public arena, then we will have no voice in the nature of the multispecied universe of which we are a part.

Laurence Rockefeller was in favor of disclosure, as was James Forrestal. (There has always been some confusion as to how Forrestal died. He was either pushed or jumped from his hospital room window after a depression relating to the secrecy of the entire project.) Laurence Rockefeller founded an initiative in the early nineties that resulted in a report that was distributed to the U.S. Congress and to policy makers around the world. I met with Laurence often about his desire to compel all governments to disclose fully all information on UFOs and E.T.s.

Of course, the politics of disclosure would change the very nature of how we define ourselves as humans: scientifically, religiously, psychologically, and philosophically. Even with all of our other Earth-plane problems, it seems to me the time has come to ask for help in acknowledging their presence. According to the latest polls here in America, 80 million people believe they are here and know our government is lying to us. We know we need restructuring of our military intelligence. Why not make this part of it?

Since there is concrete evidence that the public wants to know, it is my belief that disclosure would not foment fear and hysteria. The fear of a dishonest government already exists. We need an educated public in order to debate the biggest issue of our time. The movement toward a world civilization is inevitable. Shouldn't we be educated and prepared to be a part of that civilization? Other countries do not employ the government secrecy that ours does. Students debate their presence, as do the newspapers. Why are they here? Where do they come from? How long have they been here on Earth? What do they want?

We need to be agents of change so that we can participate in a cosmic reorganization of life. We need a star being paradigm shift so that we can be part of the new and peaceful world regardless of our differences.

# chapter

## 9

I'M IN MY CLOTHES CLOSET UNPACKING GARMENTS THAT I have kept for twenty-five years or more. I can remember where I got each item and feel the emotional charge it still holds. That's why I can't part with the clothes I love. In fact I'm going to ask the wardrobe department people from my new picture *Poor Things* to come here and shop in my closet for what I'll wear on-screen. I could clothe ten pictures from this closet.

Sometimes when I have my past life recall, I can actually see what I and others around me wore. Maybe that's why I'm so tied to the emotions of clothing. I am not a fashionista. In fact, quite the opposite. I've been on the worst-dressed list most of my life. But do I have stories to tell about being comfortably shabby!

I am tired at the end of a day of organizing my closet and setting up my new office, but Terry seems as full of energy as when we started. She seems to love her new home and is finding all manner of secret places to hide. I wonder what invisible energy she sees that is not obvious to me. The office is adjacent to my bedroom and overlooks the terrain below as though it is an eagle's nest. I sit and watch the sun as it sets over Los Alamos and find it ironic that Los Alamos means "the trees." I remember that Oppenheimer called himself the Destroyer (Kali) for making a nuclear weapon, and I wonder how many trees have died as a result of his bomb.

I am happy with my life right now, but I do feel old. The older I get, the more I think about God, more about my life's meaning, more about what we term consciousness. My friend Chris Griscom, a healer and past-life therapist, and I have conversed often about how our genetics and our DNA and consciousness merge. We talk about making a soul connection with our bodies. It occurs to me so often now that one day I will literally not have this body any longer, and I will live with only my soul memory of what my life was like living inside it. My perceptions and familiar tools of physically relating to the world will be over and gone. Someday I will look down, and someone else will be living in this house and working and thinking in this little office with his or her own beloved animal, wondering about the future of Earth.

I don't have much of a fear of death. Pain, yes, but not death. This may be the reason I am free to speculate on the truth of other realities.

At the same time I'm looking forward to what life on the "other side" will be like. I wonder if my DNA strain will be broken if I decide not to come back for a long time. Will my DNA flow through my soul memory? I'm appalled when I realize that many people ridicule or become cynically angry at such speculation. Why don't they wonder, I wonder? What could be more interesting than speculating upon who we are, where we come from, and will we come again?

Chris says that DNA is a chemical composition that is influenced by emotions and environment. If we inherit a bad temper, we've inherited that emotional DNA. We have parenting and grandparenting DNA and great-great-grandparenting DNA, etc. We even, I believe, have inherited galactic DNA (I'll write about that later). I think that there comes a point in evolutionary time when the human DNA changes. Mutations occur caused by other cosmic activity.

I feel we are in the midst of those changes now. I feel an evolutionary pulse as though much negativity in our DNA is being loosened and released. The darkness is freed, which must occur because we cannot go on the way we are. We cannot carry the negativity residing within our DNA into the future. We need to sit down together and discuss our differences, but more important—what do we have in common? We need to call forth a higher force, which we know we have in common, even though we are killing each other over that higher force.

We need to expand our capacity for togetherness, which we intuit is inside each one of us. There is another way to live, to expand our consciousness to include the commonality of our so-called enemies. God is either our commonality or our separation point. I don't think enough of us realize that the God force is within us, not outside of us. In fact it has been considered heresy to say that God lies within. I believe such a heresy has been manipulated so that some powers that be can create separation and divide and conquer. Chaos and wars mean profit to many. Therefore, suspicion, rage, and anxiety become the ruling emotions and conversations of our society. Instead, we should be having conversations about the origins of greed (materialism) and the separation from the Source. We have greed and separation imprinted on our DNA. Somehow, we have allowed ourselves to be separated by the manipulation of materialism. I feel it everywhere in the movie business, and, of course, materialism is the mark of our success and identity in our culture.

As I sit watching the gruesome results of religious conflict cross my TV screen and newspapers, I'm forced to evaluate the consequences of religious convictions relating to the definition of insanity and reality. According to the latest Gallup Poll, 35 percent of Americans believe that "God" wrote the Bible and all of it is literally true. We believe that the Lord God Jehovah said that anyone who believed in a god other than Him should be killed (Deuteronomy 13:7–11). How much of our past and present is the result of such a command? This is our world now.

The Muslim world is living the same command: "All infidels should be killed and Hell shall be their home" (Koran 9:73). We enact our human morality according to our religious beliefs. God, Allah, has promised us all heavenly rewards as long as we believe in Him. But not only should we believe in Him, we should fight for Him against those who do not believe. "Onward Christian soldiers, marching as to war . . ." "He that leaves his dwelling place to fight for Allah and is overtaken by death shall be rewarded by Allah. The infidels are your inveterate enemies" (Koran 4:95-101).

Martyrdom is the way a Muslim avoids judgment. He goes straight to Paradise. The fundamentalist Christian believes that Christ will return to Earth soon because the fighting in the Middle East is a sign that Armageddon is around the corner and the Messiah will usher in a thousand years of peace. As a person believes, so will he act.

So deeply embedded are these religious beliefs that talking together to resolve differences seems unreligious. We don't really have freedom of religion. We have religion that is free to do anything in its name. We believe in these religions with no real evidence. We only have the "belief" that facts are there. Many of us are quite willing to martyr ourselves for beliefs that we have no evidence for, Christian and Muslim alike.

The Hebrew definition of belief is "the assurance of things hoped for and the conviction of things to come."

When I was in China and the Soviet Union twenty-five years ago, I saw the authoritative governments practice a form of political religion on their people—a political religion called Communism, while professing to ridicule the "opiate of the people" in the West. Their political religion martyred millions.

The Old Testament required heretics to be put to death. During the Inquisition the book of Deuteronomy served as a text for the inquisitional torture. It stated that even members of one's own family should be put to death if they so much as entertained the thought of believing in another God. Even St. Augustine believed that torture was appropriate for those who broke the laws of God. Later, the Christians saw the Jews' denial of Jesus' divinity as consummate evil.

During World War II, the Catholic Church looked the other way during and after the Holocaust. Not a single German Catholic was excommunicated before, during, or after the genocide of six million people. Pope Pius XII was busy excommunicating others (scholars and theologians) for holding views not commensurate with the Catholic view of truth.

Muslims are entreated to "share power with the enemies of God." The word *jihad* literally translated means "struggle" or "striving" or as in English translation, "Holy War." A devout Muslim declares *jihad* against his own sinfulness. Then an armed conflict in defense of Islam is a dutiful obligation. They, according to Bernard Lewis, "expect victory in this world as well as the next because the world will adopt the Muslim faith or submit to Muslim rule." *Jihad* is the duty of a Muslim. He who dies without having taken part in a war against the infidels dies in a state of unbelief. Paradise is in the shadow of swords. If a Muslim renounces Islam, the penalty is death. "Whoever changes his religion, kill him" (Koran 3:86–91).

The threat of mutual destruction in a nuclear world won't matter to an enemy who longs for Paradise anyway. I don't see how democracy would work in a Muslim theocratic state, and for that reason I don't understand the "democracy building" fantasy of the Bush administration. Islam, just like any fundamental religion, doesn't depend on what its "God Book" says. It depends more on what the people *think* it says. How many people devote their entire lives and energy to this invisible God, which they believe is the *only* God?

What happens, then, to a civil society if it is inundated with fundamentalist religious beliefs? And how do we stop those beliefs from fascistically running a society? It's as though we're back in Inquisition days.

When will human beings identify with human beings instead of an invisible God? It's as though we are compelled like moths to flame to rush headlong into the Armageddon that has been prophesied because of the fear of our own sins. Fundamentalist Christians support Zionism and the Apocalypse because such a prophecy would usher in the Second Coming of Christ!

I wonder what our natural human nature is. Is it basically violent or is it because we see our Gods as violent? Since the beginning of recorded time, 93 percent of that time has been spent on war! *Seven percent of all time has been devoted to peace.*

More than 50 percent of Americans have a negative view of people who don't believe in their God. Seventy percent of Americans believe it is important for a president to be "strongly religious." Most of our social issues (stem-cell research, gay marriage, abortion, free speech, pornography, assisted suicide, and even a declaration of war) are framed in the context of our Judeo-Christian theology.

When will we stop revolving ourselves and our enemies around religion and begin to look more seriously at the exercise of expanding our own consciousness? We would be able to transcend our conflicts if we understood that we are spiritually and scientifically interconnected. We would then have a paradigm shift in thinking and behavior. "Do unto others as we would have them do unto us" would shift to "Do unto others because they *are* us." We need to learn more about what consciousness really is. It has emotions, perceptions, attitudes, and ultimately worldviews that come from spiritual beliefs.

We have become familiar with the feeling of spiritual separation—separation of other members of the human race, separation from ourselves (division), separation from God (outside not inside). Somehow we've agreed that separation is natural. How can separation from the Divine Source be natural? But because of that belief, we have defined ourselves on a self-destructive level. We are killing ourselves and each other because we "believe" it's human nature to fight over territory and God and country.

Where will our perceptions of God and religion take us in the twenty-first century? Do we have to go through yet another religious crusade and war in order to truly understand that our perceptions of God are literally insane? Our Earth family constellations include members of that family we have never met. We've inherited DNA through intermarriage that expands our fixed notions of who we are and should fight to continue to be. Through our religions we are usually focused on what we should do to *feel* God . . . pay our dues, pray, feel insignificant, obey the religious laws, never relinquish our sacred territory, and obey the Ten Commandments, even though these commandments came from a God who warned that he was jealous, vengeful, and must be obeyed at *all* costs, including death and execution. It's time we got in touch with our spiritual DNA. All DNA is connected to the Divine. I believe it's time to fully understand and believe this connection or we are lost. I believe such an understanding of this truth will alter our negative DNA.

If we think and feel we are born to suffer, struggle, and succumb, then we can change our thinking and feelings. We can replace them with divine feelings of balance and contentment. We would be feeling what has been there all along. Once we find the feelings, we can hang on to them, then we change. We become more balanced. That is truly channeling one's own perfectly balanced soul. Once that happens, there is no need to fight or be angry about anything. Such negative feelings fall away, and possibly so does our negative DNA.

Living in a global society today, we can no longer hold together in this world unless spiritual (not religious) conversation becomes a part of daily conversation. We need to talk with one another about nature and beauty and the miracles of synchronicity so that we can relax and trust that there is indeed a guidance in our lives. We need to talk about the unity of our yin and yang, our soul. When we are in touch with our oversouls we are mirroring the divine. In that mirror we will find ourselves. I can't say that I've done this yet. But at times I am truly content and happy. I am without angst, which is a real accomplishment for an overachiever.

Perhaps I need to reinvent what I think of as God, which automatically means I have to reinvent myself. Perhaps that is what I'm learning and teaching myself. Obviously, the violence and killing isn't working in our world. We need to aspire now to resonate to our "better angels" within which is, I believe, our basic human nature. We need to reinvent God in a positive way that supports the highest octave of human society. Jesus, Buddha, Krishna, Mohammed, all spoke of divine love. Why are we fighting over it? Why is one person's God better than another? What in God's name is really going on?

There are those who feel we are into the "Shift of the Ages." It's been predicted by the Mayans, the Incas, the Hopis, Nostradamus, and the Bible Code. The shift is supposed to occur somewhere between the 1980s and through 2012. They say time will begin to move more rapidly; therefore, we will feel an increase in energy and electromagnetic frequency all around us. We will feel we are able to get things done more quickly. If we are not driven crazy by the speeding up of the electromagnetic frequency, we will feel more of a sense of personal empowerment.

I feel all of this is happening now. And from what I've read, it is happening as a result of our solar system moving into the Photon Belt. The Photon Belt is a belt of energy generated by what quantum physics calls quarks, neutrinos, photons, etc. All of these tiny, infinitesimal but extremely powerful particles of light illuminate the un-solid, un-physical world. You might say they cause an illumination of the Spirit World. Our solar system passes through this Photon Belt of light particles every twenty-six thousand years. Apparently, we entered this belt in the early 1980s and will be going through it for a thousand years. The photon energy frequencies accelerate everything. They accelerate understanding, awareness, self-knowledge, and the *primal* understanding of the Divine Energy itself, which means . . . they also accelerate confusion, chaos, anger, and negativity. I believe that is what we see accelerating. We are having a healing crisis. When that crisis subsides, I believe we will begin emotionally to feel that we are all one and that we are divine as well. Because of this crisis and acceleration, karmic issues will become resolved. We will go through a healing process, which will also be extremely painful because we will be detoxing, releasing and cleansing pains, aches, traumas, psychological terrors and fears, hatreds, anger, and desperation.

So, in effect, every twenty-six thousand years the buildup of emotional and karmic toxins is cleared. We will seem to experience a disintegration of our Earth cultures and feel that the world is coming to an end. But in truth, the cleansing of negative karma is necessary and positive so that we can go on to a new world of light and love. I call it Karma-geddon. Instead of Armageddon, a Karma-geddon will be occurring, which will be the resolution of all our karmic issues down through the ages. Therefore, yes, the world will shed the old ways of living and come into a new life of peace and happiness. This is not unlike what the Book of Revelation portends when it says that after Armageddon, we will have one thousand years of peace.

# chapter

10

BECAUSE OF MY AGEING AND THE QUESTIONS IT POSES, I
think a lot about the future and what I'll miss if I decide to go
soon. Knowing me, I'll want to stick around for the action, whatever it might be—so I'm thinking a lot about the prophecies.
Should we believe the prophecies? They have been with us since
recorded history and they are fundamentally the same . . . there
will be cataclysmic Earth changes, wars and rumors of war, pes-
tilence, starvation, disease, all leading to the elimination of two-
thirds of the Earth's population. In short, the end of life as we
know it. Not necessarily the end of life on the Earth, but certainly
not what one could describe as a bright future.

"All the armies of the world gather at Meggido [Armaged-
don] and unite; as they go to move on Jerusalem they become
consumed by a sacred flame," says the Book of Revelation.

I ask, is the sacred flame a nuclear blast from star beings
who find our human behavior finally too insane? Is it a nuclear
flame from one of Earth's armies as we come into the End of
Days? Would the stopping of a military campaign against Jeru-

salem by star beings be considered participatory or interference? Is it an unconscious synchronicity that is meant to happen? Must all human players come together to determine whether there will be the destruction of life as we know it or one thousand years of peace, which Revelation also prophesies?

I have been to Meggido (Armageddon) several times. It is a field now, quite a beautiful landscape of Earth, which used to be an ancient fortress along the trade routes. Meggido has been the focus of many ancient battles and, therefore, the place where ancient armies developed the world's first peace treaties. It is fitting, then, that Meggido would be the focus of potential peace treaties now.

From Revelation to Edgar Cayce, Nostradamus, Isaiah, Matthew, and the Dead Sea Scrolls as well, all portend a future of despair and apocalypse. However, there are alternative realities prophesied also—one thousand years of peace, cooperation between people and the angels of Heaven, and a great healing for all the peoples of the Earth. It's our choice, they say.

Ancient prophecy has haunted us for millennia, taken from ancient texts found in the Middle East, Tibet, South America, Mexico, the American Southwest, and in the psychic minds of those who claim to see the future.

Gregg Braden has examined one of the ancient texts called the Isaiah Scroll. It was written more than five hundred years before the time of Jesus and was discovered intact among the Dead Sea Scrolls in 1946 and resides, well preserved, at the Shrine of the Book Museum in Jerusalem. I have seen it. It is unrolled and mounted upon a vertical cylinder. It is considered irreplaceable, of course, and is designed to retract into a steel vault in case of a nuclear attack.

Through Gregg Braden I discovered its meaning. Isaiah describes a future world completely laid to waste and utterly stripped of life. This description is not unlike the Hopi prophecy, as well as that of the Maya of Mexico. The Gospel of Matthew says, "There will be famine and earthquakes from place to place. But all these things are the beginning of the labor pains."

The Native American elders claim their ancestors predicted there would be four cataclysmic changes upon the Earth. These were ages of ice, water, fire, and shaking. The Mayan calendar says we are at the close of the fifth Sun, which coincides with the Aztec calendar that calls it the fifth World. The common predictions for this time are unusual weather patterns, loss of coastlines due to rising sea levels, famines, drought, earthquakes, and the breakdown of global infrastructures and law and order.

More than a few twentieth-century seers predict massive Earth changes, which include the breakup of the West Coast of the United States, a great inland sea connecting the Gulf of Mexico with the Great Lakes, the submerging of much of the East Coast of the United States, lands rising from the Atlantic Ocean, the submerging of most of Japan, changes to the northern part of Europe, volcanic eruptions, and a polar shift that will alter all climatic conditions resulting in certain temperate and semitropical areas becoming tropical.

I have been sent world maps from Gordon Michael Scallion and Lori Toye, who see these images as visions, but they don't know each other. The maps are quite specific and quite alarming.

The Book of Enoch states that he has heard all things and understood what he saw, which will take place in the distant future. In these days the rain will be restrained (drought), the fruits of the

Earth will be late and not flourish in their season (that's happening now), Heaven will stand still, the moon will change its laws and not be seen at the proper time period.

Edgar Cayce saw Earth changes all over Europe, the East Coast of the United States, the West Coast of the United States, and the Mississippi running in the opposite direction. Others see a consortium of scientists detonating a nuclear explosion to take the pressure off the tectonic plates . . . a mini ice age in Europe . . . glaciers freezing Maine . . . two years of rain, and a nuclear bomb exploded in the Middle East just as an experiment.

Rather than run off in fear of what I've just described, I have a different take on the prophecies, namely Revelation. First of all, Armageddon may have already happened—several times. My hope is that *we* won't be the reason it happens again. A new Jerusalem could be just around the corner. What if St. John the Divine wrote Revelation as an acknowledged blueprint for man's consciousness? What if the seven churches and the seven candlesticks and the seven seals are a description of each individual's seven chakras, which produce a healing crisis when confronting our own divine nature? All the prophets underwent their own pain and suffering when looking within to their personal conflicts. Perhaps that is what we need to do in order to achieve a New Jerusalem and an ensuing thousand years of peace. If we each looked into the depth of our soul and brought about a union of mind, body, and spirit, there would be no reason for conflict whether within ourselves or between one another.

When a critical mass of citizenry is reached, those people would be the residents of a New Jerusalem. If one-third of mankind were to make that internal change, we would have a different world. We would, through our in-depth searching, realize we no longer need to live out the karma of Atlantis. We would balance our lifestyle with our new consciousness.

In interpreting prophecy, I sometimes wonder if the predictions from a "higher" psychic intelligence aren't predictions, but are really a larger PLAN. A plan to call people to a better way of life. Perhaps the predictions do not constitute the end of humanity but are more a blueprint for the potential of the human race. Perhaps they are there for us to see the positive potential instead of emphasizing the negative, which we have done down through the sorrows of the ages of our human race. We know there is a yin and a yang to everything. We know that if we have light, we simultaneously have shadow. Life is the balance of both. Instead of fearing the shadow, we could use its teaching beauty. We don't need to be such a reactionary species. We each need to take personal account of our own shadows. From that point of view, Revelation and every prophecy, for that matter, is a cautionary tale as well as a potential blueprint.

Perhaps the in-depth investigation that each of us invokes will open our seven chakras (seven energy seals) and will give us more awareness of what we are really doing. We will then each have a crisis of consciousness, which is long overdue. As Socrates said, "An uninvestigated life is not worth living." Or as Yeats said, "The only journey worth taking is the one through oneself."

The seven churches and seven candles are, I believe, a methodology of opening the energy centers in each human being. We must each do the individual work for ourselves now. No church or state can discover what we will know about ourselves; therefore, they can't direct us any longer. It is a simple matter to take the time every day to stop all activity and meditate (focus) on the seven energy centers within the SELF. Just acknowledging that they are there causes an opening. The more acknowledgment, the more opening.

When the first base chakra (the fight-or-flight energy center) is open, we take more accurate evaluation of what it is that frightens us. When the second chakra (the sexual creative energy center) is open, we understand more accurately what we are doing or not doing with our sexuality, and therefore our creative expression becomes more balanced. When the third chakra (the personal power energy center) is open, we are more fully in touch with our sense of control and how threatened we are if and when we don't have it. The ego mechanisms of the third chakra become less maniacal and manipulative.

When the fourth chakra (the heart chakra) is open, we become more compassionate, loving, and sensitive to others. It is also the resting place of the soul itself. The heart chakra of nearly every human being I know (except for children) is fairly well closed because of fear (first chakra) and concern for personal power and welfare (third chakra). When the heart chakra is open, one must be prepared to have a more trusting nature and all that such trust involves. But the dividends of having a high value for trust in one's life gives us a heart-centered intelligence, and using that condition wisely is a consciousness-raising growth process.

When the fifth chakra (the throat chakra of communication) is open, each person speaks his or her own truth, and it is no mystery what progress we could make in the world if truth were the means of communication, even when there is dire disagreement. When the sixth chakra (the vision center in the middle of the forehead) is open, the vision that each person has for peace in the world and for his own life can be more fully realized. Visions are thwarted these days out of misconceived necessities. If we can visualize something, we can make it happen.

When the seventh chakra (the energy of our spirit connected to God) is open, we feel we are indeed guided and protected by the loving power of our creator, and if our intention is pure and in service to our better angels, we feel we will never be harmed.

So to me, the seven churches, seven candlesticks, and seven seals are about the potential power we all possess to make a New Jerusalem blueprint for peace in the world. The opening of the psychic centers does not have to result in negative consequences even though it will be painful: The truth of oneself usually is. It is more like a homeopathic crisis that intensifies the symptoms for a while before a healing occurs. A fever always precedes a healing, because it is a sign of fighting off disease. We are all suffering from dis-ease. The dis-easement of the spirit. The dis-easement of knowing who we really are and, more to the point, who we can be.

It is everyone's individual decision to have as much healing as we are willing to receive. The Bible says that 144,000 of us will be "taken up." That is a critical mass number for the healing of mankind. Perhaps 144,000 human beings will "see the light" of themselves and change everyone. If we wake up soon enough, we will have what St. John the Divine prophesied as a thousand years of peace.

The word "apocalypse," taken from the Greek word *apohalupsis,* has a seemingly innocent definition, meaning to disclose or reveal. In that definition we can see what is meant by the Prophet John of Revelation, saying that man has turned his face away from the angels and forces of the Heavenly Father and the Earthly Mother and has therefore fashioned his own destruction.

When John asks if there is any hope, a voice replies, "There is always hope for you for whom Heaven and earth are created."

It was then that he saw a different scenario. ". . . My vision changed, and I saw a new Heaven and a new Earth; for the first Heaven and the first Earth had passed away. . . . And I heard a great voice . . . saying . . . there shall be no more death, neither sorrow, nor crying, neither shall there be any more pain." As his new vision continued, he saw no need for war, and mankind would live in peace. A voice guided him: "People living in those days will determine how they experience the great change of humankind's future."

The Hopi also saw a possibility for living in peace and joy.

In the Essene Dead Sea Scrolls are written important scientific facts that have been confirmed. The air in our lungs is the air over the Earth, and the water, of which we are 90 percent, is the same as was once the oceans and the mountain streams; therefore, the Essenes implored us to see ourselves as one with the Earth rather than separate from it. (I often think of my time in China in 1973 when my guide pointed with pride to an industrial plant whose operation had turned the natural stream next to it to sludge. It was his pride of conquering nature that was so upsetting.)

The Essene scrolls go on to say that the Earth outside of us only mirrors the self inside: A polluted Earth means a polluted inner self. As inside, so outside. Hence, problems with our immune systems. Our consciousness is so disturbed that nature is mirroring us. Nature follows mind: therefore, earthquakes, disturbed weather patterns, drought, famine, etc. We humans are the custodians of the health of Mother Nature, not the other way around. So the state of our world is a reflection of the state of our human beingness.

The prophecies seem to be unfolding on time. Melting ice caps mean rising seas, rising seas mean submerged coastlines. Quantum physics gives us the hope that there are many outcomes for any given scenario depending on the free will of our choices today. We have to create the reality of our future now.

Stephen Hawking told me, "In the quantum world, each action by each individual counts. We are in a world where we create together. There are no hidden agendas if we would just look."

Above the desk where Hawking works in Cambridge is a picture of Einstein and Marilyn Monroe. "When I look at the curves of the universe," he said to me, "they are each equally beautiful." With tears in his eyes, he said, "Anyone who thinks I don't believe in God hasn't heard what I've said. I'm just not sure that God is necessary!"

According to Hawking and other physicists, if we redirect our focus and attention to something new, we would bring a new course of events into focus. Therefore, a consensus of predictions can be altered by a new consensus of focus. We need to rewrite our future. For too long we've put our power to sleep in favor of a more material focus. Nowhere is that more obvious than in Hollywood. Everything in Hollywood is about money, marketing, ratings, box office, and "success." But what is the definition of success? The art of expressing human conflict and emotion in order to know oneself (character-driven films) has taken a very long backseat to hardware, special effects, horror, and sex. We are definitely, it would seem, in show *business*.

The materialization of this beloved industry is not contributing to the growth of the understanding of humanity anymore. It is contributing to the bank accounts of those who have pirated the vision of film in the first place. And it is contributing to fear.

Because of the audience nonacceptance quotient, everyone is afraid. Not many stalwartly defend their original vision anymore. It is a shame—and I am ashamed. No wonder I look to quantum physics, prophecy, mediums, and New Age philosophies to help me understand the meaning of life. Hollywood certainly isn't helping much.

Ageing through Hollywood is not a good move anymore.

That's why I live in the Land of Enchantment, not the Land of Enhancement. I feel the difference the moment I leave my soul place and find myself on a freeway in Los Angeles, which most of the time is a parking lot. I try to direct my thoughts to the "meaning of life" but find that I'm forced to think of survival instead.

Survival cannot be solely what I should be concerned with. The evolution of my consciousness, my understanding, my compassion and my cooperation with nature, and the evolution of my human expression on film should be on my mind as I move about my life. I am happy and grateful to still be part of the film business, but my heart and mind are heavy with the priorities and the money people hold so dear out of fear.

At a Hollywood party I long for conversations about human progress and where we are going in a cosmic sense, but the introduction of such subjects promulgates embarrassment and fear. It's as though conditions in our world have deteriorated so completely that no one wants to engage in its alarming meaning for fear that they won't be able to erase it from their minds. "Let's not talk about this," I hear. "It's making an imprint on my mind that might be long-lasting. That's why I don't watch the news or read the newspapers anymore. Let's enjoy ourselves." We will talk about politics and the science of winning and losing. We will even discuss politics apropos the nature of freedom and democracy and material corruption. But will we discuss politics in relation to our separation from the Founding Fathers' spiritual intent? No! It seems we feel politics has nothing to do with our spiritual separation and corruption. We still think in terms of spirituality being religious. It matters not that wars over religion and God are what might catapult us into nuclear destruction.

Are we talking about fiddling while Rome is burning here? But worse, is everything happening just as it should? In that case, do we have the president (W.) and the administration we deserve? Do we need to be staggering in denial until we are virtually in the gutter before we seek a higher power of enactment? We don't even want to be part of a participatory democracy if we don't understand that we came from Founding Fathers who were more interested in the meaning of spirituality than religion.

Spirituality includes the science of light and time and intention. What is our intention these days? To have peace? Peace isn't only the absence of war. It comes from within so that it can be studied without. Peace, to me, is just being, not striving toward the next goal or desired success or political victory. Peace is finding happiness in small things. Peace is feeling one with all things. Peace is the freedom of curiosity to speculate on any possibility. Peace is being able to question the accepted political agendas of society without worrying about what people think. Hell, I don't know—peace is my warm puppy to cuddle up to at night.

So, if I address myself to a new and different intention of political focus, perhaps the agreed-upon prophecies will not come to pass.

We need a new synergy and a new truth eliminating the demonization of our enemies as we are being demonized by them. We need to become evolutionaries, which means we've progressed from revolutionaries. Radical individualism often ignores people with needs. Radical collectivism becomes a military totalitarianism. We need synergy that will become a new truth.

Our Founding Fathers learned democracy from the Iroquois Indians. The Iroquois lived as part of and within nature. They worshipped the Great Spirit and understood its ways. We need to adhere to our own principles as set out in the Constitution *around the world* so that we are champions of everyone becoming a universal human. If we are the New Atlantis, we need to understand the mistakes of the past so we are not "condemned to repeat them." We need to understand our spiritual and psychic ley lines and vortices.

When I walked the Santiago de Compostela Camino pilgrimage, I felt the energy of walking along those ley lines. They were energetically educational. I learned things about myself I didn't think were there. I went into some past-life experiences, wrote about them, and went through a healing crisis of my own. I've been on a Camino ever since.

I can feel the polar shift unfolding, which only means that the sacred vortices are moving in accordance with the procession of the equinoxes. Climate changes are the result. But the changes are more confusing and disturbing because we are out of touch with the natural evolution of nature. It becomes a shock to us and is literally more shocking than it needs to be because our consciousness is so contaminated and polluted.

Perhaps we should look at the karmic prophecies more as dharmic prophecy. Dharma means "the energy that does the work." I call dharma "spiritual service," which I like to feel I'm doing. When we are aligned with our dharma, we use energy to serve. I think I serve myself and others when I do a good job acting or performing or writing. When I use "the energy that does the work," I am then an individual in the service to the collective whole. Then, in appreciation, the collective whole serves me, the individual, and I go on serving the collective whole again.

As an individual, I love to study mystical and metaphysical points of view on history. I already know what I was taught in school, which was basically HIS-story. So I am deeply interested in whether we are the New Atlantis, as Sir Francis Bacon believed, or why Sir Isaac Newton's deepest interest was in decoding the Bible, which he believed contained a code buried in its text. Newton made complex drawings of what he saw as the New Jerusalem and intricately studied crystals, which he believed would be the new source of energy. He believed Jerusalem was a sacred geomancy vortex that was to be a model for peaceful living. Perhaps he believed that the journey of the people of Israel would be an example of mankind's journey, which would eventually be the reinvention of itself. We would organize our societies around energy principles, not principles of money and conquest. Democracy would become a universal thought instead of an excuse for capitalism. And in crisis we would look within for what concerns us and why it does instead of being afraid of what's inside.

Clearly, science is seriously investigating the relationship between nonphysical reality and the effect it may have on what we call physical reality. What is this invisible force that Einstein and others concluded holds the physical world together? "A spirit of superior intelligence," Einstein called it. Or as Louis B. Leakey put it, "Without an understanding of who we are and from where we came, I do not think we can truly advance."

I think we stand at a moment in time when the survival of our humanness depends on our ability to marry the observance of the invisible force with the forces of our actions.

The Essenes suggested that we have forgotten the lost science of prayer. Gregg Braden and John Hagelin write that prayer transcends science, religion, and even mystical traditions. They correlate prayer with the forces in quantum physics. They claim that the energy of collective prayer with the agreed-upon intention could alter the prophecies.

Again and again in the Bible Code are encrypted, along with the prophecies of gloom and doom, the four words in Hebrew: "Will you change it?" The Bible Code also suggests that we play a significant role in the outcome of predicted events. The words "Will you change it?" presuppose a being who asks the question. Who would that be? And who wrote the Code anyway? Its accuracy is alarmingly consistent. How could the first five books of the Old Testament (the Torah, which has been unaltered through time) have embedded in its text a code that portended the future thousands of years ago? It's as if the writers saw a future technology able to unlock its warning when we would need it.

Ancient prophets said we had the ability to change the future by the actions we take in the present. The question now is—are we waking up to what we've become too late?

Einstein said time does not flow in only one direction. The future exists simultaneously with the past. There is a connection within physics between time and prophecy. Time is the major factor in the way we lead our lives, but because we see time as linear, we are frustrated with not having enough of it. There is an ancient school of thought that the present and the future are knowable *now*. It's difficult for me to understand that, *but* I can imagine it. Such must be the quantum physics inherent in prophecy. If a person's mind is holographic enough, he or she can tap into the ALL and, therefore, see the "future." That must be what Hawking meant when he told me there was never a beginning (a Big Bang) and there will never be an end.

Being an invalid who can't move at all, he must have inner capacities to see universal time in its true sense. Was this the case with Edgar Cayce, John the Divine, Mayan and Aztec prophets, and the writer or writers of the Bible Code? If they were immersed in the universal time and "God" energy, perhaps that is why they also understand that a communal intention of feelings could change an outcome. Hence, communal prayer.

I met with John Hagelin and the Maharishi Yogi's people concerning just that. They claimed that through massive collective prayer meetings they reduced crime in a given city or even altered the weather. It's called the Maharishi Effect.

Is the secret, then, that we must work on our intentions communally and together? How will we know if we get an answer? They say, "Don't pray for world peace—*see* it. Don't think of it as the opposite of war. Such a thought gives too much power to war." The Maharishi, Hagelin, and Braden are seeing and evolving their ideas in the same way.

The science of "determinism" (German philosopher Gottfried Leibniz) says that everything witnessed or experienced in this world, regardless of its random appearance (accidents), happens because of the events that preceded it. To me, that is not quite the definition of karma, but close.

In quantum physics, "free will" enters the equation. We change everything by observing it. Quantum physics is the study of radiating light waves (quarks, photons) and nonphysical energies which, when we move them, create our physical world. Therefore, if we moved the nonphysical photons and quarks within the action of intentional prayer, perhaps we could change the physical outcome of prophecy. This implies the possibility of multiple outcomes for an event that has been seen to have already begun.

We used to be told that it is scientifically and physically impossible for two objects to occupy the same space at the same time. Quantum physics has proved otherwise. It is called the Bose-Einstein condensate, named after the authors. If two future events are seen simultaneously, even for a second of time, then one can move past the other and become the future reality in a "quantum leap." If our invisible universe (God) is what holds us all together, why couldn't we intentionally appeal to it to create an outcome we not only want but learn to "see?"

The Essene Gospel of Peace says, "In the moment of breathing in and breathing out is hidden all the mysteries." Tiny changes of free intention can lead to gigantic changes of presupposed outcome. That means we need to change the way we express ourselves in the present. We have parallel possibilities in anything we do in life. The chaos of our world is a wake-up call to examine what our own self-meaning represents and what we want for the world.

The *feeling* in prayers, not the words, is what influences the unseen universe. We breathe life into the prayers through feeling. They say we need to *feel* that what we ask for is already there. It is that silent language of feeling that allows us to become portals through which Heaven can pass to Earth. Hidden in the mists of our ancient time, we each have a memory of this silent, powerful language that connects us to one another, the cosmos, and Heaven itself.

It seems that my course in life has been to use expression in dancing and acting to explore some of my questions relating to human identity. I'm fascinated by the character and motivations of people. Why do we do the things we do? Why don't we long more to explore the invisible power of the universe within us? I've been mystically inclined as long as I can remember. I don't know where it came from, except for the aforementioned characteristics of my parents. I only know I get more pleasure from asking questions than anything else in life. I accept very little at face value, yet I'm a trusting innocent who believes that there's some truth in everything.

People who know me say I have a low bullshit quotient and a high bullshit detector. So it has been confusing for many of my acquaintances that I believe in so much that I can't see. The search for visibility is worth it. The absence of evidence is not evidence of absence. Some of my searching and incessant questioning has not been easy, either for me or those who know me.

The Lost Gospel of Thomas explains it best for me.

Let those who seek continue seeking until they find.
When they find, they will become troubled.
When they become troubled, they will be astonished.
Recognize what is in your sight, and that which is hidden
from you will become plain to you.

# Chapter
# 11

PEOPLE WHO LIVE IN NEW MEXICO SEE MANY "AWE-INSPIRING phenomena" in the sky, especially if they live at as high an altitude as my house is (eight thousand feet above sea level). As I've said before, I've always been interested in whether there is "life out there." I sit alone on my eagle's-nest balcony and wonder if maybe tonight I'll again see the same kind of phenomena I saw when I was in Peru. There, as I watched alone from my eighteen-thousand-foot-high lookout post, craft darted across the sky night after night, seemingly to tease those scientists below with their telescopes and recording devices. People come from all over the world to record and witness these events. It is common conversation in the Andes that people from other worlds come to our world to mine our minerals and observe us.

How long have the other-world beings been with us? Could they have actually been written about in the Bible? I go to my library and open the old Bible on my desk at random. It "accidentally" opens to 1 Thess. 4:16–17: "For the Lord himself shall descend from heaven, with a shout with the voice of the archangel, and with the trumpet of God. . . . Then we . . . shall be caught up together with them in the clouds, to meet the Lord in the air; and so shall we ever be with the Lord."

My mind goes to the Pillar of Cloud that guided the Israelites by day and the Pillar of Fire by night through their forty years in the desert. I had always wondered about that, too. That led to hours of reading the Bible (particularly the Old Testament) from the star-being point of view. I found it extremely exhilarating and intriguing. Had star beings been with us from the beginning?

Who were the gods of the Bible? I say gods in the plural because "gods" in the plural was the original translation, unlike the King James Version. I wonder what else has been altered from the Great Book since its inception.

As I read many books on the subject I began to agree that there is sufficient evidence that the human race has been influenced by beings far superior technologically to us. There is ancient evidence of their influence in art, science, genetic engineering, harvesting, soul science, mathematics, and in general many areas of life that propelled us forward far faster than the speed by which we would have progressed alone. Yet in the process, we humans seem to have learned, by proxy, many "divide and conquer" techniques, because that is what seems to have been visited upon us.

There are a myriad of stories and myths in every culture that tell of great wars in space, the battles between light and dark forces, the gods of heaven. In fact the Bible predicts another "war in heaven" "as above, so below." Titanic struggles which have already occurred on Earth between the Gods of Light and Dark are due to occur again. Has the struggle back to divinity always been filled with such polarity violence?

The Bible is filled with descriptions of heavenly chariots, sky-born pillars that spit fire from heaven, clouds that dictate commandments and wheels within wheels which transported humans (Ezekiel) from one location to another on Earth in the space-time of minutes. The Ramayana of India describes a double-decker hovering craft with a dome and portholes. The vimanas of Krishna's time were flying fortresses that threw laserlike arrows at humans and exuded light that melted the very skin and teeth of the cowering humans below.

The Egyptians and Damans each described shields of fire. Alexander the Great spoke of shiny shield-shaped objects with beams of light that attacked his enemies. Many flying shields have been described today and in the past which fly with the speed of light. In the Bible the Nefilim are described as those who came from heaven to find the daughters of man fair. "Nefilim" means "one who fell down from heaven" and are sometimes interpreted as "fallen angels." Most of the gods were called "watchers" or "warners" and were sometimes referred to as angels. If we are being visited by star beings and in fact are inheritors of their influence, I would like to know. It would help explain our historical behavior and progress.

I have slept in the sarcophagus of the King's Chamber of the Great Pyramid at Gizeh, and I'm certain it was built by minds and spirits that were not human. The Great Pyramid is perfectly aligned to true north, and the three pyramids together on the plateau are in the same configuration as the three stars in the belt of Orion, a constellation that is mentioned several times in the Bible. In 1985 NASA discovered an identical configuration of the three Gizeh pyramids on Mars. The pyramid was constructed as a giant sundial indicating the precise dates of the solstices and equinoxes, dividing the time not only into years, months, and days, but even by hours. The weight of the pyramid (now estimated as being 5,955,000 tons) when multiplied by one trillion equals the modern scientific estimate of the Earth's own weight. The circuit of the base of the Great Pyramid divided by twice the height of the pyramid produces π (3.1416). Pi is a mathematical constant representing the ratio of the circumference to the diameter of a circle—elementary geometry. Archimedes, who lived two thousand years after the pyramid's construction, was given credit for discovering π, which was key to many mathematical calculations. So the architects of the pyramid possessed precise knowledge of the movements of the Earth, the laws of gravity, and the existence of π. There is also a fascinating school of thought that says that all of human history is recorded in the pyramid—dates and events can be interpreted mathematically through the interior system of passageways and chambers.

I've stayed through the day, and well into the night, at Angkor Wat in Cambodia, which mirrors the constellation of Draco as it appeared in 10,500 B.C. I have gazed at the Nazca lines in Peru which are ancient, and the configurations can be seen only from the air. The giant spider on the Nazca plains is a replica of the constellation of Orion. Why are these structures and ancient artifacts erected on specific ley lines, namely, between the thirteenth and thirtieth parallels on Earth? Who made the cuttings with laserlike precision in ancient stone megalithic structures in Peru, Yucatán, Mexico, Indonesia, and Mesopotamia (Iraq)?

The ancient Sumerians were proficient in advanced mathematics, predicting the future positions of heavenly bodies, and advanced energy medicine. They developed advanced astronomical calendars good for 25,720 years (the return of the zodiac is every 26,000 years). Their astrologers worked with a finely tuned sense of the psychological and spiritual impact that the zodiac had on the human mind. They had advanced architecture and other various sciences that date back to at least 65,000 years ago.

All of this has been translated from hundreds and thousands of Sumerian cuneiform tablets, many of which were located in the museum at Baghdad and stolen during the American invasion. Why would anyone who invaded steal such priceless objects unless there was an interest in the advanced meaning of the translations? The seat of the most advanced ancient civilization was Sumeria (Iraq). It makes me wonder what we are really doing there.

There was a great leap forward in the Sumerian civilization in architecture, astronomy, philosophy, medicine, and knowledge of the cosmos. Many independent cultural stories about the origins of civilizations indicate that the knowledge came from non-human sources: "gods," "watchers," "teachers," "Nefilem," and "those who travel in sky-boats." The Old Testament is full of these stories. Enoch walked with "gods" and was instructed by them. Noah learned of the impending flood from one of the "gods," named Enki, who instructed him to build the ark. Ezekiel walked with the "gods" from whom he received the plans for the temple at Jerusalem. He even left the Earth in one of their fiery chariots as they taught him sacred geometry. And then there is Jehovah, who not only guided the Israelites for forty years in the desert but became quite cruel and upset with what he considered their sins and transgressions against him. "I am a jealous and vengeful God," he reminded them and dictated the Ten Commandments to Moses from a pillar of fire in a stentorian voice. The serpent god gave prohibitive instructions to Adam and Eve in the Garden of Eden.

Like Krishna in the Bhagavad Gita, the messages from the gods were dictatorial, yet practical, prophetic, and technologically spiritual in nature. If Adam and Eve were the first and only people on Earth at the time, why was their son Cain so afraid to leave Eden lest he be slain by "everyone" out there? Who was "everyone," and who were the people in the "Land of Nod on the east of Eden" where Cain went? If I were writing a screenplay on this subject, I know the audience would have questions until it made sense. Why were the pharaohs of Egypt called "gods"? Were they offspring or descendants of the sky "gods"?

The Koran speaks of a race of people that existed before those of us who were created from dust. They were called the "Jinn" race. The Koran goes on to say that "Allah created humans from dust, then from a sperm-drop." The ancient Mayan scriptures (The Popul Vuh) teach that four different kinds of humans were created through genetic engineering to serve as slaves for the "gods." Who were the gods? And if we didn't serve them well, what happened to us?

The Indian Book of Dzyan talks of a serpent race coming from the skies to help mankind with medicine, DNA, and light on the planet. I wondered why the medical staff of the caduceus was two serpents intertwined. Why is the snake dance of the Hopi Indians in the Southwest the most sacred? Why did Moses set a "brazen serpent upon a pole"? Why were pharaohs depicted riding on the backs of flying snakes? And why do the Chinese claim that their royalty came from their celestial dragon ancestors? Who were the dragons?

From an inspirational point of view, is there a bloodline that has been inherited down through our history and has dictated intermarriage in "families" to preserve our inheritance from the stars and to ensure their control? Are we humans basically someone else's property? Are we controlled by those who wish our planet to be used for their own purposes rather than by our own free will? And more to the point, what *is* our free will? Is it a subterfuge granted to us in the belief that we will never understand that we are and always have been controlled by what we refer to as gods?

We seem to have a variety of star beings represented as having visited the Earth: Lyrian, Sirian, Orion, Zeta Reticuli, Pleiadian, Arcturian, Andromedan, Cassiopian, and Ganymede. There seems to be a "celestial peacekeeping force" that guards our solar system from others but is prevented from protecting us from what we do to ourselves. They give us spiritual warning (through our intuition, etc.) and do what they can to prevent nuclear holocaust.

As I've said, I have seen the craft darting across the skies in the Andes of Peru as they seemingly land and take mineral samples and other ecological specimens to monitor what we are doing to Earth. Some have contacted government representatives on Earth concerning a policy of disarmament, but have been rebuffed, because we are deathly afraid of each other due to our own fundamental feelings of distrust. We thoroughly mistrust the motives of the star beings, who we fear may want to destroy us. I wonder if the star-being mistrust comes from the genetic memory of how cruelly they treated us long ago. Just as there are a variety of human beings to deal with, perhaps there are a variety of star beings to deal with, and perhaps our challenge now is to become sophisticated in our discernment of who is light and who is dark.

As I've already researched, there is evidence to substantiate that Jehovah was a star being and also that there were other star beings who attempted to have dominion over the Israelites before him. The six-pointed Star of David existed long before Abraham and seems to indicate that there were six other star-being "lords" before Jehovah. One could have been Melchizedek, who was called the god of all gods, the unseen, unmanifested father who resides at the center of the universe. Another star being could have been Seth, who taught salvation by understanding the nature of reality. His teachings took root in Egypt and spread throughout Europe, Asia, the British Isles, Japan, and the Middle East.

Some of the great star beings are said to have written many of the Old Testament Psalms and inscribed them on stone slabs. The references to god in many of the ancient texts did not refer to Jehovah at all. They were called "Nazarites" and were in existence long before Jehovah. The Nazarite sect existed long before the laws of Moses. The Persian word "Nazaruan" means "millions of years." The Nazarite mystery schools are said to have taught the Osirian teachings of Atlantis and civilizations even earlier. Many of these teachings have survived in India and in the Hermetic schools of Egypt. Some have also survived in the mysteries of Freemasonry and some in the teachings of Pythagoras and the Kabala.

The teachings of the "unknown god" also survived in the ancient pre-Vedic teachings of India, which I was privileged to have been told about by Prime Minister Jawaharlal Nehru when, years ago, I visited India for three months. Once, as I attempted to swat a fly near me, Nehru held my hand back, saying, "Do not kill this creature, you do not know who it might have been." What Nehru was describing is what is called "the transmigration of souls," which means that a soul can reincarnate into a species other than human in order to work through its karma.

I'm not sure what I believe in relation to that. But now would be a good moment to discuss the subject of reincarnation in general. I have written about it a great deal, to little avail where my Western friends are concerned. Or rather, they don't seem to want to talk about it publicly like I do. Maybe they're right where their careers are concerned, but where the laws of karma are concerned, I think it's essential. Even Christ taught that what one sows, so shall one reap. It's simple. What we put out returns to us. It's called the law of one, or the law of return.

In the Kabalistic faith, reincarnation has been recognized for centuries. The school of prophets as established by Samuel and Elijah taught reincarnation, as did the Essenes, a sect of which Jesus was a member. It was also taught by Origin, the Greek philosopher, and by the early Christians until A.D. 325, when twenty churches met at the Council of Nicea. There and then they adopted the new doctrines of purgatory, Hell, and the Trinity. The existing references to reincarnation were either changed or discarded.

Later, in A.D. 553, at another Council of Nicea, arranged by the Emperor Justinian and his wife Theodora, entire books of the Bible were renamed and the belief in reincarnation was declared a heresy and punishable by death!

It's interesting to me that Edgar Cayce claimed to have the specifics on the lifetimes of Jesus. He said the soul of Jesus had previously incarnated as Amilius in Atlantis 108,000 years ago, Adam, Enoch (also known as Thoth/Hermes), Melchizedek, Zend, Ra (in Egypt), Joseph, Joshua, Asoph (seer for King David), Jeshua. As Asoph, Cayce says he wrote many of the Psalms of the Bible.

In the year 1607 King James selected fifty-four people who were well versed in the language of the Old and New Testaments to make a new translation of the Bible. It took them three years, and that version has come to be the one many of us know best. However, the Old Testament mentions many books that have been lost: the book of Jasher, Book of Gao, Book of Jehu, Acts of Solomon, Book of Nathan, Visions of Iddo, Prophecy of Ahijah, Lamentations of Josiah, Shemaiah the Prophet, Chronicles of King David, and Book of the Wars of the Lord. I would very much like to read that last one.

The doctrine of the physical reembodiment of the soul is the only thing that makes sense to me in relation to cosmic justice in life. What we reap we must surely sow; what we put out returns to us, as all energy follows the laws of science. In this case a spiritual science, which is why science exists in the first place—to prove and explain the existence of the spirit.

To return to the existence of the "gods": There is evidence that there was rivalry between them. Jehovah summed it up when he declared that he was a jealous and vengeful God, and we humans should have no other gods before him. There must have been many different star beings and many different levels of hierarchy in the councils of the "Divine." Are we humans confused and loath even to examine our confusion because we want so deeply to believe only in the one unseen God of all? Star-being "gods" are seemingly responsible for initiating this thing called "religion" (to bind) so that they can have control over not only binding us humans, but also have the power to divide us and thereby, whenever it suits them, conquer us.

I think of the works of Jehovah in relation to the Arab-Jewish conflict: "To me belongeth vengeance for a fire is kindled in mine anger, and shall burn until the lowest hell, and shall consume the Earth." Jehovah is often described as a "consuming, devouring, refiner's fire" who moves about inside a "fiery throne." (Exod. 16:7–10, 24:16, 40:34–45; Lev. 9:6, 23, 10:3; Num. 14:10, 21, 16:19, 42; Deut. 4:24, 5:24, 9:3; Kings 1:10; Chron. 7:1, 3; Job 1:16; Ps. 18:8, 29:3, 72:19, 89:36, 97:6; Isa. 4:5, 6:3, 10:16, 17, 29:6, 30:27, 30:31–9, 49:4, 66:15; Jer. 48:45; Ezek. 3:23, 8:4, 11:23, 43:2–3, 35, 10:4, 18; Dan. 7:9–10; Joel 2:3; Hab. 2:14; Mal. 3:2; Heb. 12:29.) He told Moses he used "lying spirits" to achieve his territorial goals and that vengeance belonged to him and that Moses should keep his people in fear of his anger. David himself sang songs to Jehovah, the lyrics of which were: "The Lord is a man of war"; and in Job we read: "The glory of his nostrils is terrible . . . he swalloweth the ground with fierceness and rage."

The books and chapters and verses describing the rage and violence of Jehovah are too numerous to rcitcratc here. Let it suffice to say that the "Lord God Jehovah" had some problems, and it does not sound as though he was a god of love who Jesus said was the truth of the unseen God in the New Testament. So perhaps the human race came under the influence of a star being called Jehovah who was himself a defective "fallen angel" and influenced us accordingly. Perhaps if he had acknowledged more the feminine aspect of himself (even star beings are made up of yin and yang), he wouldn't have been so threatened regarding his need for absolute power.

Each human culture creates or worships its own god in the image it is either taught or desires. The result is that there are as many "gods" as there are cultures. Conflicts and wars easily follow. Followers of Christianity, Islam, and Judaism agreed that Jehovah was their God, a "god" who was antagonistic to all other gods. Call it Jehovah, Yahweh, Allah, or whatever, the God of Abraham was believed to be the one and only God to Islamists, Jews, and Christians. And each of the cultures had a different idea of who and what this God of Abraham (Jehovah) represented as the supreme and primal force in the universe. Each culture has been inhibited and emotionally confused, producing antagonism and anger toward one another, which could have been the psychic technique used by Jehovah, Yahweh, Allah, and the God of Abraham in the first place: to pit one tribe of humans against another in order to maintain control. We humans have been deeply disturbed in our consciousness ever since. Who is God? Will he forsake us? Does he feel we are sinners and will we go to hell if we don't do his bidding? Are we having such problems in the world because *we* deeply believe we are all sinners?

With this attitude deep in our subconscious and ruling the consciousness of our earthly societies, how can we possibly mature into self-realized and loving human beings who understand our own loving inner power? The word "god" or *deos* in Latin simply means "being from the sky." What about the deos in our own hearts?

The Egyptian Pharaoh Akhnaton made an attempt to move his culture away from the god-cult mentality. The "gods" from the skies were preventing, in his opinion, the more sensible integration of man with his natural environment . . . the natural order of the universe. He attempted to gain acceptance that the Sun was the source of our power on earth, substituting it for the sky beings, which we see replicated in so many Egyptian hieroglyphics. This experiment got him assassinated but his "non-star-being god-cult" ideas remained accepted in esoteric circles.

The one great master who espoused the notion of the Divine God within and not the Divine God without was Buddha. His advocation of inner focus and the disciplines of the power of human divinity within provided the human family with a way of perceiving itself as being connected with the creator and not separate from the god source. His teachings are not considered a religion. They are considered a divine philosophy.

These teachings were also the teachings of Jesus. "The Kingdom of Heaven lies within." He went on to teach that every son of mankind is equal to the sons of God ("star beings"?). There is much evidence that Jesus spent the missing eighteen years of his life learning in the esoteric schools in Babylon, Persia, Egypt, and India, where he studied the teachings of Buddha. He was known as Saint Issis. No wonder his ministry antagonized the Sanhedrin (Orthodox Jews), the Romans, and the temple leadership in Jerusalem. The disciples of Jesus, after his crucifixion, continued his teachings but with variations and numerous interpretations of his original message. Most of them lost sight of his original truth. One group, the Gnostics, seemed to retain an understanding of his democratic and humanistic God-within approach.

His original teachings spread to Greece and the surrounding areas, only to give way later to god-cult forms of dictatorship that employed supernaturalism again as its belief system, a kind of magical view of sky gods as their saviors until, after the Council of Nicea in A.D. 325, we had a kind of dictatorial supernaturalism of Christianity, which was based entirely on faith: a nonbeliever being unable to test his or her views against the believer.

As most of the "civilized" world in the West and Middle East came under the influence of the magical supernaturalism of the doctrine of the religious WORD, there were small communities that tried to preserve their freedom of thought, intuition, and emotional independence. I belong to one of these unnamed communities—the community of myself, whose doctrine emphasizes personal responsibility, the value of each individual, and a love of the Creator and those star beings who want to help us, not divide us. I am not a Freemason but I agree with much of what our Founding Fathers (many of them Freemasons) decreed as their beliefs and values in founding this nation. They did not believe in the Divine Right of Kings. They believed in the search for increased knowledge of the universe, recognition of the rights of the individual, the practice of self-determination over a religious-oriented autocratic government, and the practice of social equality.

As I've said before, I come from Virginia, the home of eight presidents, many of whom were transcendentalists as well as Freemasons (sixteen of our presidents have been Freemasons), and I believe that each of them would applaud and agree that my search for the real meaning of our human history is worth it and well meaning. I don't know what they would think of my star-being theories, but I do know that many of them were interested in "life out there."

In my research, I was pleasantly surprised to discover that many of our early Colonial and American leaders' libraries were stocked with authors such as Emanuel Swedenborg, Fontenelle, Huygens, and William Derham. Each of them wrote on "the plurality of Worlds and the beings who lived there."

Benjamin Franklin wrote often on his sense of awe and speculation. "Great God," he wrote, "what a Variety of Worlds hast thou created! How astonishing are the Dimensions of them! How stupendous are the Displays of thy Greatness, and of thy Glory, in the Creatures with which thou hast replenished those Worlds! . . . Who can tell what Uses those marvelous Globes may be designed for."

In 1728 he wrote:

I believe that Man is not the most perfect Being but
One, rather, that as there are many Degrees of Beings his
Inferiors, so there are many Degrees of Beings superior
to him. Also, when I stretch my Imagination thro' and
beyond our System of Planets, beyond the visible fix'd Stars
themselves, into that Space that is every Way infinite, and
conceive it fill'd with Suns like ours, each with a Chorus

of Worlds for ever moving round him, then this little Ball
on which we move seems, even in my narrow Imagination,
to be almost Nothing.

In *Poor Richard's Almanac* for September 1749, Franklin wrote,
"It is the opinion of all the modern philosophers and mathematicians that the planets are habitable worlds." In the middle of a letter to a friend explaining his own hypothesis about magnetism, he
wrote, "Superior beings smile at our theories, and at our presump-
tion in making them." To another friend he expressed the wish
that the friend's idea of happy conduct might "grow and increase
till it becomes the governing philosophy of the human species, as
it must be that of superior beings in better worlds."

The diary of John Adams (a long-ago ancestor of mine, I'm
told), who became the second president of the United States, also
contains references to other solar systems. On April 24, 1756, he
wrote, "Astronomers tell us, with good Reason, that . . . all the
unnumbered Worlds that revolve round the fixt Stars are inhabited, as well as this Globe of Earth." That day and the next, he
went on to reflect upon whether all the "different Ranks of Rational Beings" in those worlds had committed moral wickedness, and
if so, whether any church leaders would think they must be "con-
signed to everlasting Perdition." It is evident that he himself did
not think so.

One of the more remarkable figures in Colonial and early
America was Benjamin Banneker. Born in rural Maryland in 1731,
the descendant of slaves, early on he demonstrated extraordinary
mathematical and analytical abilities, along with a photographic
memory. Between twelve-hour shifts on the family farm, young
Banneker, without the benefit of formal schooling and with lit-

tle more than a handful of borrowed texts as his guide, achieved excellence as a mathematician and astronomer, and honed an elegant writing style on par with the finest writers of his day. Later in life, his self-taught expertise as a surveyor led to his playing a pivotal role in planning Washington, D.C. And his *Banneker's Almanac*, first appearing in 1791 and continuing as a best seller for years after, was celebrated for the accuracy of the celestial movements it provided navigators and its weather forecasts, as well as its humorous anecdotes, philosophical essays, and extraordinarily fine prose and poetry.

But Banneker's most remarkable achievements were in the field of astronomy. Long before the Hubble Orbiting Telescope, he hypothesized that the unusual changes in the light coming from Sirius, the Dog Star, could be attributed to the now-established fact that it is actually two stars in orbit around one another. More than a century before technology enabled astronomers to confirm that many stars are circled by planets, Banneker wrote of "extrasolar" planets that were probably inhabited by sentient beings. And his speculations about light and the relative nature of time anticipated Einstein's thinking by more than a century.

Perhaps more clearly than anyone else of the time, Thomas Paine realized that the existence of a multitude of worlds (and, thus, of extraterrestrials) was entirely incompatible with Christianity: "To believe that God created a plurality of worlds at least as numerous as what we call stars, renders the Christian system of faith at once little and ridiculous and scatters it in the mind like feathers in the air." For those who attempted a reconciliation of such plurality with Christianity, Paine warned that "he who thinks that he believes in both has thought but little of either." Paine, convinced of plurality, chose to follow the philosophy of deism.

Thomas Jefferson, despite his great and articulate interest in science, did not say much about extrasolar planets in his writings, but the catalog of his library shows that he owned the books on plurality of worlds by Fontenelle, Huygens, and William Derham, so he must have thought about the subject. Once, in a personal letter, he spoke of the "new scene" presented by the thought of planets orbiting variable stars. Jefferson wrote his own Jeffersonian Bible, flailing at the failed concepts of Christianity.

I spent the night once in his bedroom at Monticello and could feel his energy as I read his Bible. I fell asleep under the loft he shared with Sally Hemings and, when an electrical storm woke me in the middle of the night, I felt he wanted me to pay attention to the questions of the universe he had asked himself so deeply and so often. I reached out and touched his glasses as they lay on the traveling desk where he wrote the Declaration of Independence.

The next day the curator of Monticello gave me a lock of Jefferson's hair, which safely resides in my home in New Mexico. I was asked to surrender it for DNA purposes to prove the lineage of offspring between him and Sally. But I wouldn't part with it. Jefferson's DNA is not far from me, ever.

The guards at Monticello claim they watch Jefferson walk and whistle as he surveys his grounds late at night. They have made recordings of his presence which, of course, make sense to me. So to me . . . Jefferson lives.

Several of the Founding Fathers believed in the ongoing journey of the soul, which with each physical reembodiment, the soul is engaged in learning.

If we made a transition from supernaturalism to natural spirituality, I believe we would become a more peaceful race of beings who would integrate ourselves more lovingly with not only each other and with Mother Earth herself, but also with the recognition that we are part of a galaxy of celestial beings who have been learning their own lessons just as we are.

I have read all of Zechariah Sitchin's work as well as that of William Bramley and Paul Von Ward. Each of them has concluded that, according to the Sumerian cuneiform tablets, our human race was seeded by beings called the Annunaki, whose home world was a planet called Niburu. Sumer means "the land of one who watches." In the fifth millennium B.C., the Sumerians built great cities, organized a system of city-states, used the wheel for many things, had a monetary system that used gold and silver as its standard of values, a system of credit with interest, a calendar based on lunar months (thirteen, not twelve), a study of the stars, a system of weights and measures, medicine and advanced surgery, radiation treatments, the use of petroleum products, water control systems, reservoirs, domes, vaults, and the arch.

The gods of these highly civilized Sumerians were a trinity from the planet Niburu. According to the translations from the cuneiform tablets, the "gods" were called "Din Gir" (Din meaning "bright," Gir meaning "rocket"). The home of these gods was "E. Din." The gods from Niburu traveled in sky vehicles, wore helmets with goggles, ruled as divine kings from on high, and were termed Royal. The Egyptian word for "divine" means "one who watches."

According to the Sumerian cuneiform tablets, the trinity that ruled Sumer were Anu (seen as the ultimate divine authority in heaven); Enlil, the god of earth; and Enki (also known as Ea), who was known as the god of water. There were also fifty deities who were "sub-gods" from Niburu who helped rule the Sumerians and lived among them. My research indicates that the Annunaki were assigned (by whom I don't know) the Earth territory known as Mesopotamia (now Iraq). There were other gods upon the Earth from space who were assigned other Earth areas to develop. All of this preceded Jehovah by hundreds and thousands of years.

Nearly every tradition on Earth describes gods (by different names) who were descended from the heavens in marvelous awe-inspiring machines, and with magical powers they intervened in the development of human life. They set up dynasties, had sexual intercourse with humans, taught advanced technologies, and in the case of the Annunaki in Sumer, engaged in genetic engineering to develop a human who would serve as a kind of mining slave for them. Apparently, according to the tablets, the Annunaki needed powdered gold to shoot into their home-world atmosphere that no longer protected them from the radiation rays of their own sun. This was their mission on Earth and the Sumerians even looked upon themselves as the property of the Annunaki gods because of the advanced technologies they were also being taught. They saw themselves as workers on a divine estate.

Most creation myths around the world involve the presence of powerful beings from the sky, and nearly all allude to the gods from the sky creating and developing the genetic engineering of mankind from the beginning. Sumerian texts suggest that Adam (the first human) was incapable of procreating. Therefore Eve was "created" in order to multiply. According to Paul Von Ward's research from the cuneiform translations, there were parallel scenarios throughout world cultures. Legends from the Andes region in South America describe the "creator gods" traveling between the heavens and the sea while "making" humans on the Earth. The Arawak tradition of the Caribbean says the sky-being creators Kuramany and Kulimina created man and woman. The Andean account attributes the creation of humans to plural gods.

Genesis states that the gods (Elohim) formed man from the dust of the earth. The Quiche translation says the Elohim made man from clay. In India a Vedic myth says the creator gods used the power of light and water in creating the Earth and its creatures. As Von Ward questions, "Does this mean that there were prehuman creatures before *Homosapiens* as the fossil records indicate?" Both the Australian aborigines and the Dogon in West Africa claim their oral traditions go back sixty thousand years. Both groups believe their first ancestors were the result of magical acts by male and female beings who came to Earth from the skies.

In the American West the Selish tribes claim that a god creator used hair from his head to create the first five women. The Quinaults of the Pacific Northwest believe their "changer god Kinatle" created humans from his own sweat. These gods were said to come from the sky. The Chaco tribe from the Pampas in South America say a female named Kasogonaga, hanging from the sky, created humans. The Algonquins and the Blackfeet of North America say their god (Kiei Manitu and Rapi, respectively) made man from the Earth with a breath of spirit. The Norse traditions recorded in the Eddas report that humans were created from two trees (ash for male and alder for female). The trees symbolized the tree of life and genetic knowledge.

This all suggests, according to Von Ward, that these widely separate cultures date from the beginning of the Annunaki creation but were left out of the subsequent experience of the Annunaki colonial culture that came later.

As I remember my past-life experience in Atlantis, I recall that the civilization in Atlantis was highly advanced, was in cultural exchanges with star beings, and there were *many* star beings, some of whom may have been the Annunaki. There seem to have been many "sky gods," however the Sumerian cuneiform tablets relate to the Annunaki.

There is much research to suggest that the Greek accounts of the Titans, the Demi-Gods, Homer's epic poem *The Odyssey*, the Gods considered to be from Atlantis, Titan offspring, and the granddaughters of Uranus and his Earth wife, Gaea, are basically accounts of the progeny of sky beings intermarrying and having sexual intercourse with Earth humans whom they genetically engineered to be more developed and advanced. Some original humans apparently had star being parentage. The "Last Book of Enki" as translated by Zechariah Sitchin includes details of the genetic engineering of "prehuman" species already existing on Earth. The details are much the same as the biological, cloning, and genetic engineering we read about today: the manipulation of human eggs, star being semen, blood from each, and dust and clay from the Earth. All these manipulations contributed to our DNA and their DNA as a result of their offspring.

Sound far-fetched? Consider a fascinating article by John Stokes published in the newspaper *The Canadian*. Stokes reports that a group of researchers working at the Human Genome project have revealed that they have made an astounding discovery: They believe that so-called noncoding sequences in human DNA (sometimes called junk DNA because it does not contain instructions for making proteins or other cell products) is no less than the genetic code of extraterrestrial life-forms. Noncoding sequences are found in all living organisms on Earth, but in human DNA, they constitute a larger part of the total genome, according to Professor Sam Chang, the group leader. After much analysis, the researchers were forced to wonder if the apparently "junk human DNA" was created by some kind of extraterrestrial programmer. This would mean that every life on Earth carries a genetic code for our extraterrestrial cousins.

In Edgar Cayce readings, he portrays Atlantean humans as having been seeded by the gods. He says a lower form of human with more of an animal nature remained after the sky beings' seedings. Cayce says they served as beasts of burden and slaves for the more advanced beings. This is essentially what the Lost Book of Enki says. Enki, as I've said, was one of the triune Sky Gods from Niburu. I have always been interested in where the idea of "Divine Right of Kings" originated. According to the cuneiform tablets translation, the Annunaki were thought of as sky-god kings, so to speak. Whenever they appointed a subordinate to take charge of something, he was commissioned with the power of the divine gods. He ruled with the "divine right of a sky king." This practice has been handed down for thousands of years. A king rules by divine right because a star being long ago represented himself and his commissioned rulers as divine. The new kings, human or otherwise, were apparently ordered to preserve their bloodlines by carefully considering their genetics before producing offspring. Therefore: royal bloodlines.

What is Niburu? According to the Sumerian cuneiform tablets, it has an elongated orbit and every 3,600 years it passes near our sun and inner planets. Its inhabitants are the Annunaki (in the Bible: Anakim). It is approximately twenty-five times larger than our planet and has a gravitational pull that corresponds to its size. If its orbit occurs every 3,600 years and such a passing results in Earth cataclysms, great floods could have happened as a result.

There is much speculation as to Niburu, of course, even as to its existence at all. But something disastrous occurred 3,600 years ago that could have been the end of civilization as we know it and the beginning of another. The question is how do these celestial events fit in accordance with what science tells us about the reasons for the ice age, floods, and the presence of advanced sky beings who must have known and been able to warn humans of the impending disaster then. Were superior civilizations inundated by the cataclysm of the return of Niburu? And did the Annunaki help with rescue efforts in any way?

The cuneiform translations say that Enki informed the likes of Noah, thereby saving some humans. The Lost Book of Enki claims that his triune brother Enlil had begun to detest the human experiment and wanted the race of engineered humans annihilated. Being a sky being from Niburu, Enlil knew of his home world's return to Earth and simply allowed the unspeakable destruction to occur. His brother Enki felt differently, apparently, possessing more compassion than Enlil, and informed not only Noah, but other humans as well. It is unclear in the tablets whether the Annunaki removed themselves for a time (or were removed by the celestial council) from Earth after the Deluge. However, it is recorded that many humans were desperate for rescue, instruction, and more devotion to the Annunaki so they could survive and reestablish what they had before. The humans had never conceived of life without their divine rulers and were now on their own. Anyone prophesying the return of the sky beings was revered and listened to, so desperate were the crippled humans for help. Anyone suggesting certain forms of behavior in order to ensure the return of the divine ones collected many followers. Thus the birth of belief in the Second Coming, celestial signs, Earth changes, more cataclysms, personalities who would possibly prevent the return (anti-Christs) and much desperate, rageful violence. It is said in the tablets that sometime after the cataclysm, other sky beings as well as the Annunaki returned to Earth to establish new civilizations.

Supposedly the Annunaki publicly apologized for allowing the Deluge to occur without warning, and efforts with other sky beings began to progress. The level of sky being support in the Middle East is recorded in the tablets without identifying specifically who they were. But the Bible discusses the sweet influence of the Pleiades, the bands of Orion, and the presence of Arcturus and Sirius. The level of support to humans seems to have been based on precataclysmic relationships, even hybrid family ties, offspring, and lists of genetic genealogy. The Atrahasis texts record that the Sky Gods, led by Sud and Ishtar, wept over the plight of the humans as they watched from their sky vehicles. Sitchin translates in "The Wars of Gods and Men" that the Nile Valley was reclaimed for human habitation by Enki. The Sinai Peninsula was the place selected for the Annunaki postdiluvian spaceport, which included a space control center on Mount Mariah (the future Jerusalem!) From these geographical areas the sky beings would focus their efforts, which would birth the three seminal civilizations whose combined influence would shape what is known today as the birthplace of Western civilization. First came Sumeria (Iraq and surrounding area of Mesopotamia), second Egypt, and third, Israel. The Bible seems to corroborate this thesis after the Flood.

A series of gods, demi-gods, kings, and pharaohs ruled over the complex social structures that began to develop. Babylon rose above all other cities and ruled from the Persian Gulf to Syria in the north. As we know, Babylon's civilization is legendary with its palaces, sciences, arts, and mathematics. The Code of Hammurabi epitomizes Babylon's level of civil society.

In Egypt, the sky beings supplied a comfortable lifestyle. Their public buildings, palaces, and tombs were unlike anything ever seen before. We know a great deal about that time period because they had a system of writing from the very beginning. Its history and culture influenced Eastern Mediterranean cultures in ways that exist even today. The female in the early Egyptian cultures enjoyed independence, power, and attention and even erotic tenderness. This sophisticated society lived less than five thousand years after the Great Deluge. Sitchin reports that for one thousand years there was peace. Then from that time on there are records of the humans involved with the Annunaki squabbles and conflicts among themselves. They fought, according to the texts, over the control of the space facilities. According to Sitchin there was a peace conference, the Annunaki were reassigned (yet again!), and new facilities were built. After some time the humans began to think of themselves as gods and built the Tower of Babel as an example of their own desire to travel in space and consort in the domain of the gods. The Annunaki retaliated by using mind control to confuse their understanding of each other's language.

Continuing with Sitchin's understandings, the Annunaki gods resumed direct rule in Egypt after the Deluge. By 3350 B.C. there developed a chaotic period in Egypt, where it was divided into upper and lower kingdoms, and humans assumed rulership as Pharaohs. Soon they, too, began to refer to themselves as divine kings since they were descendants of the Sky Gods. Thus, through infighting, Egypt went into decline.

Indian, Roman, Sumerian, and other accounts describe wars among the gods. Six thousand years after reestablishing their presence on Earth, the Annunaki were still fighting among themselves for power, interfamily influence, and territorial imperatives. I've read most of the cuneiform translations and the behavior of the Annunaki is tragically adolescent, abusive, and destructive. Their manipulations of sexual activities with families and power abuse with their own relatives and offspring make our progress as humans today look mature. Then the Annunaki royalty made a catastrophic decision. They authorized the use of radiation weapons to settle the struggle for the control of the Sinai space facility. The Near East became a nuclear wasteland and from that desolated region came a line of Abraham's descendants who would later come under the control of the God of Abraham, who I believe could quite possibly be an Annunaki sky being called Jehovah. Abraham was a Sumerian-born aristocrat. According to Genesis, he was the son of Tehar, a Sumerian descendant of Noah's son Shem. According to Von Ward, Abraham and his wife, Sarah, may have been descendants of demi-gods (Annunaki intermarriage with humans). Abraham's career seems to have been guided by Enlil and his son Nurta, supported at other times by another sky god whose name appeared later as Yhuh. Yahweh and Jehovah are determined to be the same god.

Jehovah told Moses "I am who I am." He said he was the same god that ruled over Abraham, and he demanded total loyalty in order to liberate the Israelites. He said he was to protect them from other gods and he would develop their society if they remained completely loyal to him. Jehovah apparently distanced himself from other Annunaki and their social and sexual practices. Neither did he associate with the humans. He always remained invisible and taught that doubt of him was not to be tolerated and devotion to any other god punished.

The Israelites then became a theocracy devoted to Jehovah. Depending on their behavior, the Israelites would either be blessed or cursed. They learned to obey his laws strictly, hate what he hated, and felt eternally grateful to him for "protecting" them. Jehovah ordered terrorist acts against other Annunaki and was actively hostile against women. The men were to undergo circumcision, and everyone was to wear correct clothing and perform his prescribed rituals. There is no record of his having female companionship. By all accounts he assumed the attitude of a patriarchal, authoritarian, rule-oriented Annunaki space commander.

I've wondered so often whether I lived during any of the past events I've described. Do I feel they could be fairly accurate because I was there? That time could be thousands of years ago or, if Einstein and company are right, it could be totally now, both times happening concurrently. This is the reason I love being around my animals and surrounded by nature where I live. I could watch my dogs, particularly Terry, for hours and hours. At the moment, she wants to go out. She loves to hike with me on the trail I have hacked around my house. It flows up and down the sides of the mountain. Terry seems to have mysterious agendas as she sometimes bounds ahead of me, then hangs back for some reason I can't figure out. Sometimes I get confused because I don't want to step on her. She will suddenly stop and gaze up into my eyes. I feel all time happening at once when I look into her eyes. She is the epitome of present and yet has a memory of "long-ago happenings" that I see in her eyes. Terry is not cursed with the ambivalence that afflicts us humans. She never lies about anything. Even her circuitousness about stealing food is somehow honest. I love her clarity. It is good to be around because she will be there with me, never *pretending* to be happy or sad. Whatever she is feeling permeates her whole being. She is utterly sincere, and what she is feeling is on the surface. She rarely shows signs of self-pity unless she wants to elicit attention, particularly when there is a baby around diverting attention from her. Regardless of how she is treated, she seems to overcome the experience and emerge once again with an attitude of wanting to love and be loved. I am so in awe of that attitude because it gives me hope and reminds me of something I have lost somewhere in my evolutionary past (Atlantis?) and wish to reclaim. Terry is the reminder of the unity I used to feel when I was whole. Terry, in fact, can live easily in two worlds, mine and hers, and sometimes I feel she lives in the long-ago past as well as the present. I am learning to. She reminds me of another time, which I long to know again. That, with memory, is becoming easier with advancing years.

I think Terry feels cosmic love. She seems to forgive anything and everything, even though she remembers being hurt. She lives in a state of being where judgment or anger don't exist. The past, present, and future are irrelevant to her. She has her moods, but she is always present and interested in everything and anything new; she is perfectly content to be who she is. She doesn't torture herself with alternatives or concern about bad choices and worry. She seems to love being a dog although often she seems to feel she's a person. Her emotional generosity has no limits. Cynicism is not a concept for her. Nor is she worried about how she is perceived. She definitely wants to please, but her dignity forbids her going too far. At those moments, she looks like an Egyptian priestess.

I have taken her to parties and gatherings (sometimes frowned upon by the hostess). You would think an alien had landed; "She should be tied up in the backyard," some thought.

But she didn't stand around wondering if she was witty enough or whether she was wearing the latest styles or whether she had anything thought-provoking to say. She always goes straight to the point and jumps up, in greeting, on a lady wearing a stylish black dress and pearls. For that she is fawned over and petted with endearing terms of childish cries . . . or not. Either way, I'm sure Terry comes away from a sophisticated party with more pertinent information about everyone there than the human beings who attend. She is a searcher for the authentic core of another's being and doesn't care if she is perceived as naive.

This is why we older people should have dogs. It helps us to go into hyperlove, and love is what ageing is all about. It is time to do away with self-deception, ambition, judgment, pettiness, and self-consciousness. With a dog around, you learn intimacy with yourself and a deeper capacity for friendship. Every minute is forever, and every "ever" is a good feeling. The most treasured pleasure for me is to lie in bed cradling Terry and sometime during the night wake up to realize that we might possibly be having the same dream.

As Kafka said, "All knowledge, the totality of all questions and answers, is contained in the dog."

During my "age-ing" years of spiritual "sage-ing," some of the most valuable experiences I've had have been the sessions of past-life recall. I've previously written about many of what I feel were past lives of mine, and I have found the journey of my soul through these lives very enlightening as to who I am today. When I realized that I had had many, many lives, many, many births, and many, many deaths, I stopped taking this life so seriously. There are many lessons to learn, many ways to learn them, and the soul is always intact and ready for the next advancement or life. In the past-life sessions sometimes I found myself crying (sobbing, actually), sometimes laughing, often awestruck and always aware that my own Higher Self was connecting me again with something I had already lived so that I could know more about who I really am and, frankly, move on.

If I were able to be hypnotized, I think I would make more progress, but somehow in this present lifetime I want to be in control of what I know and when I knew it! As we know, past-life therapy is being used by many accredited psychiatrists and psychologists to unhook more chronic conditions in patients that seemingly have nothing to do with the social or familial environment of their lives as children today in the present life. There are some acting teachers who employ past-life therapy so that an actor who is reticent about playing certain emotions or disturbing events can understand where the resistance comes from.

The masters teach that we have all been abusers and abusees over the course of our soul's journey through time. Life is the schoolroom, our souls the students. The curriculum is the history of who we are and have been. So past-life therapy is actually quite common in psychological treatment today.

What is not so common is the use of therapy that informs the patient of his or her life between lives. Dr. Michael Newton has hypnotically regressed over ten thousand patients, and for some reason unbeknownst to him, they all go to the experience of life between lives in order to see how they prepared and chose the next life's experience. I found that very fascinating.

It all began for Dr. Newton with one of his first patients, who was suffering from excruciating body pain in certain areas of his body. He put the patient into deep hypnosis (Newton is a hypnosis therapist) and asked him to go to the source of his pain.

Suddenly, the patient said he was on a battlefield in World War I, being bayoneted. Newton, amazed and incredulous, asked many questions, including his name, rank, serial number, date of birth, etc. The man was English. Newton later went to England to the British War Museum, the War Office, etc., and long story short, all the dates and events coincided with the patient's recall. He was receiving referred pain from his last past life in his last physical body! Newton worked with him to release the memory of the pain, and when the patient woke, he was healed.

Just as we relive present-day problems from our childhoods, we relive pain from our past-life problems. Our conscious and the unconscious mind are our finest doctors of diagnostics, if only we knew how to access the knowledge. Our souls are never at rest. They are constantly working, evaluating, accessing, and experiencing. One of the reasons we need sleep is because the soul needs to touch and connect with the unconscious to assess its experience to figure things out.

As Newton described his patients' experiences in dying, I realized I had heard nearly the same description from other people, including my own father when he had his out-of-body experience. Upon leaving his body, he said he saw a long tunnel that led toward bright and illuminating light. The light beckoned to him because it felt like his "loving home." Dad said he knew he'd been there before and was returning to "where God lives." As his soul moved toward the light through the tunnel, he said he felt a loving benevolence and was soon met by someone who told him he needed to return to Earth and finish what he came for. Most people who leave the body when passing say they are met by a favorite "deceased" relative or a spiritual teacher who either instructs them to return to their body on Earth (as in the case of my father) or leads them toward the experience of the other side and the spirit world. There is a sense of release and the understanding that its "contract" for that lifetime is finished. There is a freedom, a kind of floating feeling, no density of the heavy energy of living in a body. Then an emotion of joy ensues as they are pulled into the light. They describe it as "floating through misty veils in open space."

Most souls say there are no religious figures to greet them. Sometimes there is Christ, but usually they meet their immortal teacher, which moves them to tears. Each person said meeting that teacher again was the most profound experience they had ever had. The teacher is usually described as dressed in a white robe, surrounded by light that gives the impression of wings. Other points of light surround them until the lights manifest into guides who are there to help. They all report a feeling of "nonjudgment" regardless of their behavior on Earth, and soon they are shown the karmic reasons for their "victimhood" or abuse of others while alive in the past life.

The soul's experience then becomes one of learning because they are shown that karma itself is really an opportunity to learn from one's mistakes. They realize that they are now ethereal beings no longer tied to a central nervous system or a brain. Therefore, the "human" emotions diminish, and there is no longer an overpowering sense of grief about something because there is no longer a mind/body experience. The power of their own loving thought guides them from then on. There is no longer a feeling of disappointment in life, no longing. They are finally "home" and ready to meet new challenges with a reclaimed spiritual conscience. They begin to meet and talk with other guides and teachers. The physical environment seems to be described as a heavenly spiritual campus with quietly congregating people and temples of learning. There are temples of contemplation and music coming from the spheres with harmonic resonance. The souls say they also create what they need in this "heaven" and the guides and teachers behave according to what is needed by the soul. We are in a continual schoolroom on our journey, and always learning.

According to the patients that Dr. Newton has regressed, they say each life builds on the next one like a spiral, the soul realizing and evaluating what it needs to face and perfect. From his research, the souls say the decision to enter a new body comes after they see a fetus with at least four months of development in the womb, almost never before, because there is not enough developed brain tissue to interact and work with. The soul and the brain are two separate entities. The brain does "die" after death, but the soul is immortal. Some souls, according to Newton and his patients, don't enter the body until *after* birth.

Before entering a new mind and body, a soul peruses the DNA, the neurological map, and the karmic pattern of the family it will be entering into. A soul is always given a choice as to what it wants to experience and learn next time around. It's given a choice of bodies (male or female; many souls alternate so they can be more understanding of each).

Crib death, they say, is a karmic agreement between the new baby soul and the parents in order to learn. They come to die for the parents' learning. Yes, the new soul entering the fetus knows there will or will not be an abortion. Such an act is also for the purposes of learning. Advanced souls usually accept a future lifetime of hardship in order to learn more quickly and deeply.

For example, I think so often of the starving and abused people of Darfur, and wonder how advanced they are to have elected the lifetimes they choose. And the murdering Janjaweed—what is the lesson in the lifetime they have chosen? Could it be to horrify humanity so thoroughly that it will never happen again? Is a divine being one who teaches inhumanity as a future lesson in order to outlaw it? Dr. Newton spoke of three women who in their "heavenly" spirit world made a decision to be together, imprisoned at Dachau during the Holocaust so that they could support each other. Volunteering for a horrific lifetime doesn't occur with young souls or beginners. Advanced souls prepare for a lifetime of horror because the lessons are more difficult, and they are more prepared.

I was surprised to learn that new souls are born all the time who will need to go through thousands of lifetimes to understand who they are. There are hybrid souls who have incarnated many times on other planets (I'm probably one of these). The polarity in advanced learning is not good versus evil, but instead it is love versus fear.

Each of us has our own vibrational imprint. A soul with the same vibrational imprint is our soul mate. There is only one for each of us, and those souls incarnated at the same time know they are exactly alike in vibration and often find it difficult to live and be around each other. Twin souls are those who have elected to have many lifetimes together (easier and preferred to be around). There are also companion souls who may not have had many lifetimes together but recognize the frequency as soon as they meet. Sometimes soul mates and twin souls meet in the same lifetime and have elected to be the same sex as the other, all for learning.

Really advanced souls are androgynous because they reflect the complete and perfect balance of the yin and yang in the soul itself. Most of the advanced spirit guides in "heavenly place" are androgynous. But even they are still learning, so they will decide on a gender for the time being to learn from that. Dr. Newton said there was such a consistency to the reports of those under hypnosis that he tends to make them a scientific set of facts. The religious or social backgrounds had little effect on what they reported. Once they were in hypnosis, they were all experiencing the same method of learning.

One man reported it took him four thousand years to conquer his jealousy. He finally learned he didn't need it anymore. All of the regressed souls said their joy and freedom was boundless after death and that funerals were stupid and only for the living. "Death rituals are for those who are still in the body," they say.

Ghosts are souls who are not ready to leave. I had several of them on my ranch in New Mexico. They would open and shut doors, turn the lights on and off, scurry around in the rafters and generally be mischievous. I finally had a ceremony where I asked them to leave and reassured them that I would take loving care of the house and property. They finally did—on my side of the house. On the guest wing they still hang out, and I hear reports from my friends who sleep there. They hear chanting (I think they are Indian ghosts) and smell bread baking. Their bedroom doors (even securely locked) are open and shut all night, just to prove the ghosts are there. Ghosts are usually younger souls who are not yet ready to go on to the next level of understanding.

All of the regressed souls speak of how much easier death is than birth. With death there is a release into the light. With birth there is an entrance into density. They all say suicide is ridiculous because you never succeed in killing yourself, you succeed only in limiting the gift of learning you've been given.

The subject of drugs involved with crossing over was interesting. Drugs make the soul incapable of the beautiful experience of passing, because the soul doesn't function well on drugs. That is why they are so dangerous. Drugs basically render a person *soul-sedated*. The brain is too clouded to interact with the soul. But the drugs do not damage the eternal brain. In effect, the soul watches over our bodies, but the brain needs to be cognizant of that.

The regressed souls say that some of our myths come from spirit-memory and that when we are incarnated we still retain Super Conscious Memory. We remember the awareness of billions of galaxies and actual lifetimes on some of these galaxies if we so choose. Our planetary memory is always with us, which must be why some of us are so fascinated and certain that there is intelligence elsewhere and we have actually been a part of it. Before so much drug use in our society, we remembered more.

The regressed souls said that some souls divide to incarnate into two bodies in the same lifetime. However, that is extremely difficult because there is usually not enough spiritual energy to serve both. Only advanced souls would even attempt to inhabit two bodies simultaneously, and they do it for accelerated learning. Twins are not the same soul. They each made a decision to become twins for their own learning reasons. The more advanced souls like to alternate their sexes each lifetime so they can understand more about the opposite sex.

The spirit heaven offers no one privacy. There is no reason for privacy because there is nothing to hide. All thoughts are registered by everyone, and there is no judgment. Therefore, thoughts belong to everyone. Humor is prevalent, they say, with cosmic laughter everywhere.

I so often recall being in a huge stadium watching the Dalai Lama lecture. At seemingly inappropriate moments he would break into spontaneous peals of laughter. No one knew why, and he never explained.

The Council of Elders discuss everything in full measure and full truth with themselves and newly arriving souls. There is no compulsion to hide anything, which is impossible anyway because all thought is telepathic. Musical tones are important because they trigger unresolved conflicts and unrecognized truth. These musical tones soon become a language of communication. There are the wise ones, the wise beings. They are not angels. Angels are a religious concept. The Council members incarnate on other cosmic worlds because they are old and wise souls. They give other cosmic beings information about our Earth and vice versa.

Going before the Council of Elders who have all incarnated on other planets at various times comes as close to being in the presence of God as a soul can imagine. The energy of the Council is of such high spiritual intelligence that they seem to be in the center of the god-force itself. All regressed souls reported they couldn't "get away" with anything because all truth is known. The most important thing they learn is that intention is everything.

The concept of hell is an Earth-defined idea. It doesn't exist. All souls are held accountable but not punished. Each soul is evaluated by the continuum of his or her lifetimes, not just one. That information is stored in the Akashic Records. If a soul is unable to overcome the damage and violence he perpetuated on Earth, he is never judged in heaven; he is held accountable and worked with. Never is there the concept of blame. They said we are our own worst critics, and in the end of the learning process everyone takes responsibility for what he or she has done and is given an opportunity in the next lifetime to make amends and correct the damage.

When a "negative" soul enters the spirit world at the gates, he or she is taken to a "clearinghouse" where they enter another dimension. Hitler, for example, went to a clearinghouse dimension, as did others whose intention was so horrifyingly cruel. There is a difference, apparently, between wrongdoing and premeditated evil. The evil souls have human emotional disorders. For example, they said that Hitler was beaten incessantly by his Austrian policeman father, therefore producing basic mental warping and abnormal brain chemistry. The soul of the young Hitler couldn't handle the damage to his brain.

Hitler's soul needed energy reconstruction, which highly advanced elders help with. In the end Hitler will hold himself accountable, they said. Hitler's purpose was to incarnate again as a person who holds himself accountable. Maybe one day we will find out who he chose to be next time around.

No one soul, even the Council of Elders, knows everything. Only God knows everything. But new energy that is entering the Earth plane is loosening up our amnesia as everything moves faster.

Some of the regressed souls say they came to Earth as star beings in crafts, then decided to intermingle with humans and produce hybrids. Some incarnated in order to colonize and produce a new race of hybrid beings. Some of the souls say they came as star beings in crafts and found the Earth disgusting. Some say their own home worlds were dying. Some said they had lost contact with their home worlds. One regressed soul said he was from Orion, another from Ursa Major, another from the Gemini cluster. They said their civilizations were three or four hundred thousand years older than Earth's. They had no voice boxes because they communicated telepathically. They said that in the spirit world there is not much discussion about other star worlds. Souls stay with their own soul groups, which are defined by lifetimes of learning together. The souls on other star worlds do not fight with as much passion as humans on Earth. Passion is a challenge, they say. It can create great art, music, literature, and theater, but it can also create much destruction. *Souls come to Earth to learn the challenges of passion.* Our creativity is unlimited on this Earth school, but we must learn to be less destructive with our creativity. Some souls choose to go to fire-worlds; some go to gas-worlds.

Very high-level souls choose to come into low-level lives to achieve humility. As the Dalai Lama told me once, beware of the beggar, the janitor, the garbage person—he is probably a master soul!

I asked Dr. Newton about films and the effect of Hollywood on souls. He said the scariest film to most people was *The Exorcist* because most everyone is afraid of being possessed by the Devil. I found that intriguing and very disturbing because the writer of *The Exorcist* was a friend of mine, and we had spirited discussions about whether there was such a thing as evil. He wrote *The Exorcist* to prove to me that evil existed, and he patterned the leading lady, Chris MacNeil, after me. He even used a photograph that he had taken of my daughter on the cover of the book. I've often wondered if *The Exorcist* (which I turned down) launched me into my metaphysical search forty years ago.

Dr. Newton said we humans love the experience of being frightened as long as it's entertainment. We are attempting to figure out if fear is real or if it is taught. When we understand that fear is an externally taught emotion, we will dispense with it, and with that dispensation comes the letting go of hate. After hate goes . . . no more war.

I think we need to reconsider the whole idea of fear, especially in its Biblical context. The word most often translated in the Old Testament as fear is *yirah,* but it also means awe, reverence, respect, and devotion. The King James translators also interpreted the Hebrew *mowra* as fear, but it can refer to an object of reverence or an awe-inspiring spectacle. It seems to me that it's about time we reconsidered whether the God of the Bible is an entity who merits our fear, or perhaps instead deserves our respect and reverence. Personally, I vote for the second!

Dr. Newton said his regressed patients say that Earth is the most difficult of all the schools because our Earth plane is the plane of polarity that we see in ourselves as we attempt to understand who we are. Life has an immortal ideality we can't see and which causes fear and confusion. Therefore, we have a stream of causality going in our karmic destiny over many, many lives.

The souls said that overpopulation is a major problem, as are drugs because we live in clouded minds. They said many souls will have to leave and we are going through the equivalent of a homeopathic crisis. They said 20 percent of human souls have lived on other worlds and that Atlantis and Lemuria could be memories of these worlds. Each soul has a personal teacher and guide that has been with it since creation.

Dr. Newton said that life itself is a psycho-comedy-drama where souls literally play roles in order to understand the script called *Being Alive.* The spiritual education in the afterlife Heaven helps.

In the Ring of Destiny Selection Room, the regressed souls report there is a gigantic screen on which are projected possible lifetimes for a soul the next time around. A soul can project him-self into the screen, or he can simply observe. Some don't want to see the screen possibility at all. Guides and teachers sit with them and advise, if asked. The souls see the possible scenarios with people they either love or hate. They see dramas as to how to work out the conflicts. They see parallel universes and inter-dimensional influences. They see concurrent universes occupying the same space. They see people in the future on the screen whom they had known long ago in the past. They see pets they will be able to meet up with again. They see that all is divine and that the reason for life is to understand that.

They see people fearful because their religion has taught them they are sinners. They see spiritual libraries from the ancient days. They see the screen depicting the life they have just left. They see the world in crisis, and they see how they can help improve it.

For me, the understanding that we create, in some way, everything that happens to us was exemplified by the regressions Dr. Newton did with more than ten thousand patients. We not only create the life lessons here, we create the life we decide to lead in order to learn from them even before we're born. The first shall be the last, the last shall be the first, and it's all happening at the same time. And Earth is the most difficult schoolroom of all.

It is after dinner, and I'm sitting by the fire in my library. Terry is at my side, eating whatever I'll give her. My house feels complete, and a pleasant sense of contentment settles over me.

Last night, at just about this same time, my friends Lee and Brit Elders called me from Mexico. They were very excited and were bursting for me to hear what they had just seen.

"Carved, in ancient Hebrew, into the snow-covered slopes of Mount Iztlaccihuatl, we saw something we don't understand."

"Ancient Hebrew?" I asked.

"Yes. It was Hebrew letters and must have been carved by a craft or something high up. And as soon as the snow melted, it went away. But we have a video of it."

"What did the Hebrew letters say?" I asked.

"Well, we took a picture of it and had it translated at the Hebrew University. They said it was a phrase saying: 'On the nine the dragon will be born.'"

"What in the world does that mean?"

"We don't know, but we're doing research now," Brit promised me.

Dear Reader, let me share with you the result of our combined research into this astonishing message.

In ancient lore, the dragon has usually been associated with the chaos and conflict of consciousness. The word "dragon" is derived from the Latin *dracon* (meaning serpent), which came from the Greek word *spakelv*, which means "to see clearly."

The dragon has been associated with the darker sides of life, as has our human consciousness. The power of the dragon is often equated to an unadulterated, enlightened connection to creation, much like a newborn child who is not yet tainted with knowledge and ego. The dragon is also usually associated with the birth of consciousness, which can be conflicted and chaotic.

According to the ancient Mayan calendar, December 21, 2012, is considered to mark the end of darkness and the beginning of a new era. It also says that the human race is in a transition period between the fifth and the sixth suns. The transition began in 1987 and culminates in 2012. So we are, in effect, between two worlds now and are experiencing all the confusion and chaos that such a state of things represents.

This time is called "apocalypse" or "that which will be revealed." We are going through a shift in consciousness, and by 2012 we will have gone beyond technology as we know it. We will have gone beyond time and money. We will have entered the fifth dimensional frequency. The Earth and our solar system will come into galactic synchronization with the rest of the universe. Our DNA will be "upgraded" from the center of our galaxy.

In 2012 the plane of our solar system will line up exactly with the plane of our galaxy and the Milky Way. This cycle has taken 26,000 years to complete and, according to several researchers, two other galaxies will line up with ours at the same time. A real cosmic event!

Time is speeding up. For thousands of years the Schumann Resonance or pulse of Earth has been 7.83 cycles per second. The military have used this as a very reliable reference. However, since 1980 this resonance has been slowly rising. It is now over twelve cycles per second. This means, although it's not confirmed, that everything is happening more quickly—twenty-four hours now occur in the equivalent of what used to be sixteen hours.

During this apocalypse, people will be going through many personal changes. It is part of what we came to experience and resolve and learn.

Because of my long-standing interest in numerology, the Elders and I looked at what the year 2012 might mean. St. Augustine of Hippo (A.D. 354–430) wrote, "numbers are the universal language offered by the deity of humans as confirmation of the truth." Pythagoras, the father of mathematics, also believed that everything had numerical relationships, and it was up to the mind of man to seek and investigate the secrets of these relationships or have them revealed by divine grace.

As we looked at the statement "On the nine the dragon will be born," we came to the following conclusion. The "dragon" is our consciousness and the "nine" represents the date of December 21, 2012, as the date of change. December is the twelfth month, the date is 21 and the year is 12. 1+2=3. Add the month, date, and year (3+3+3) and we have nine! "On the 9 the dragon will be born."

On December 21, 2012, our new consciousness will be born.

# Afterword

I'M SITTING OUTSIDE ON MY BALCONY UNDERNEATH A coverlet of stars so big they look like zircons in the New Mexico sky. I'm thinking that perhaps in these pages I've tried to create a theatrical narrative that helps to explain human behavior and gives a shape to our history.

I know what I've written is intense, dense with research that is important to me, and may be exhausting to others. Yet I think that the theater of our lives is so intense and dense right now, we are badly in need of some kind of clarification and potential explanation.

Our human scripts are in need of rewrites, and we human actors, including me, need to examine our characters more deeply. Have we been playing the same parts over and over in lifetime after lifetime?

Life does seem to be a stage and each of us actors upon it. In fact, I'd say we are each the writer, director, producer, and actor in our own dramas.

The violence and chaos within our human family of actors seems beyond comprehension unless we are stuck typecasting ourselves in our scripts from long ago. I'm asking myself in a serious way if we really have engineered this material for ourselves so that we will finally become exhausted with our scenarios of war, victimization, violence, chaos, terrorism, and killing. Do we need to feel the full spectrum of the darkness we are capable of playing before we engineer the final rewrite to transition into the light of a new divine play? Is this the purpose of our tattered, war-torn end-times script?

The theater of our lives with its violent message and education may be the final act of our learning process. It is up to us to choose if we want to rewrite the present play. Or will we have to go through the theater of the violence of enlightenment yet another time?

How many times have we cast ourselves in such dramas? And what has been the role of the gods each time? Have they written us or have we written them?

I hope the disclosure of all truth will occur soon in this our theatrical illusion called Life. We've had enough cover-ups for "our protection" from the Church and State. We as human actors need to take responsibility for creating our own divine play now. There is no longer any need for manipulation for our protection.

We are ready for the truth beneath our role playing. We can rid ourselves of makeup, wardrobe, P.R., media manipulation, and marketing.

We are ready to be ourselves. Thus we will be prepared for a shift in all ways possible by December 21, 2012. We will welcome, I believe, our next adventurous journey with a clean slate and a new script.

We are the performers and the audience of our own dramas. And the show must go on!

# Acknowledgments

I want to thank and acknowledge the following people whom I've interviewed on my radio show on my website. I have learned so much from them and paraphrase them and their expertise often in my life and in this book. They are superb leaders in their fields and teachers for us all:

Frank Joseph

Carolyn Dean

Michael Salla

Gregg Braden

Zecharia Sitchin

William Bramley

Paul Von Ward

Carl Johan Calleman

Dr. John Mack

and

Brit Elders

# THE TEETH AND THE BODY

## ENERGETIC INTER-RELATIONS

**RIGHT SIDE** — **LEFT SIDE**

### Upper teeth (1–16)

| Tooth | Joints | Organs (ear/nose) | Organs | Organs | Gland |
|---|---|---|---|---|---|
| 1 | Shoulder, Elbow, Sacro-iliac, Hand, Foot, Toes | Ear | Heart | Small intestine | Pituitary gland Ant. lobe |
| 2 | Jaw, Hip, Anterior knee | Tongue | Pancreas | Stomach, Mammary gland | Para-Thyroid |
| 3 | Jaw, Hip, Anterior knee | Tongue | Pancreas | Stomach, Mammary gland | Thyroid |
| 4 | Shoulder, Elbow, Hand, Foot, Big toe | Nose | Lung | Large intestine | Thymus |
| 5 | Shoulder, Elbow, Hand, Foot, Big toe | Nose | Lung | Large intestine | Pituitary gland Post. lobe |
| 6 | Posterior knee — Hip; Ankle joint | Eye | Liver | Gall bladder | Pineal gland |
| 7 | Posterior knee — Sacro-coccygeal Joint; Ankle joint | Nose | Kidney | Rectum, Genito-urinary, Prostate | Pineal gland |
| 8 | Posterior knee — Sacro-coccygeal Joint; Ankle joint | Nose | Kidney | Rectum, Genito-urinary, Prostate | Pineal gland |
| 9 | Posterior knee — Sacro-coccygeal Joint; Ankle joint | Nose | Kidney | Rectum, Genito-urinary, Prostate | Pineal gland |
| 10 | Posterior knee — Sacro-coccygeal Joint; Ankle joint | Nose | Kidney | Rectum, Genito-urinary, Prostate | Pineal gland |
| 11 | Posterior knee — Hip; Ankle joint | Eye | Liver | Gall bladder | Pineal gland |
| 12 | Shoulder, Elbow, Hand, Foot, Big toe | Nose | Lung | Large intestine | Pituitary gland Post. lobe |
| 13 | Shoulder, Elbow, Hand, Foot, Big toe | Nose | Lung | Large intestine | Thymus |
| 14 | Jaw, Hip, Anterior knee | Tongue | Spleen | Stomach, Mammary gland | Thyroid |
| 15 | Jaw, Hip, Anterior knee | Tongue | Spleen | Stomach, Mammary gland | Para-Thyroid |
| 16 | Shoulder, Elbow, Sacro-iliac, Hand, Foot, Toes | Ear | Heart | Small intestine | Pituitary gland Ant. lobe |

### Lower teeth (32–17)

| Tooth | Organs | Organs | Organs (ear/nose) | Joints |
|---|---|---|---|---|
| 32 | Small intestine — Ileo-cecal area | Heart | Ear | Shoulder, Elbow, Sacro-iliac, Hand, Foot, Toes |
| 31 | Large intestine — Ileo-cecal area | Lung | Nose | Shoulder, Elbow, Hand, Foot, Big toe |
| 30 | Stomach, Mammary gland | Pancreas | Tongue | Jaw, Hip, Anterior knee |
| 29 | Gall bladder | Liver | Eye | Posterior knee — Hip; Ankle joint |
| 28 | Adrenal gland, Rectum, Genito-urinary, Prostate | Kidney | Nose | Posterior knee — Sacro-coccygeal Joint; Ankle joint |
| 27 | Adrenal gland, Rectum, Genito-urinary, Prostate | Kidney | Nose | Posterior knee — Sacro-coccygeal Joint; Ankle joint |
| 26 | Adrenal gland, Rectum, Genito-urinary, Prostate | Kidney | Nose | Posterior knee — Sacro-coccygeal Joint; Ankle joint |
| 25 | Adrenal gland, Rectum, Genito-urinary, Prostate | Kidney | Nose | Posterior knee — Sacro-coccygeal Joint; Ankle joint |
| 24 | Adrenal gland, Rectum, Genito-urinary, Prostate | Kidney | Nose | Posterior knee — Sacro-coccygeal Joint; Ankle joint |
| 23 | Adrenal gland, Rectum, Genito-urinary, Prostate | Kidney | Nose | Posterior knee — Sacro-coccygeal Joint; Ankle joint |
| 22 | Adrenal gland, Rectum, Genito-urinary, Prostate | Kidney | Nose | Posterior knee — Sacro-coccygeal Joint; Ankle joint |
| 21 | Adrenal gland, Rectum, Genito-urinary, Prostate | Kidney | Nose | Posterior knee — Hip; Ankle joint |
| 20 | Gall bladder | Liver | Eye | Jaw, Hip, Anterior knee |
| 19 | Stomach, Mammary gland | Spleen | Tongue | Shoulder, Elbow, Hand, Foot, Big toe |
| 18 | Large intestine | Lung | Nose | Shoulder, Elbow, Hand, Foot, Big toe |
| 17 | Small intestine | Heart | Ear | Shoulder, Elbow, Sacro-iliac, Hand, Foot, Toes |

**RIGHT SIDE** — **LEFT SIDE**

# Index

# Index

# Index

# Index